Margo
Dougicwicz

Will Bower

FOR MRS.
REIGELUTH
WITH LOVE
FROM YOUR
2015- 2016
FORM 1
ADVISEES

George Stephan

Claire Taylor

Aidarko

Sydney

Brandan DeLucia

Kate Smith

ADVISEES

Will Bower

Claire Taylor

Sydney Smith

Stephen Soares

American Cheeses

THE BEST REGIONAL, ARTISAN, AND FARMHOUSE CHEESES, WHO MAKES THEM, AND WHERE TO FIND THEM

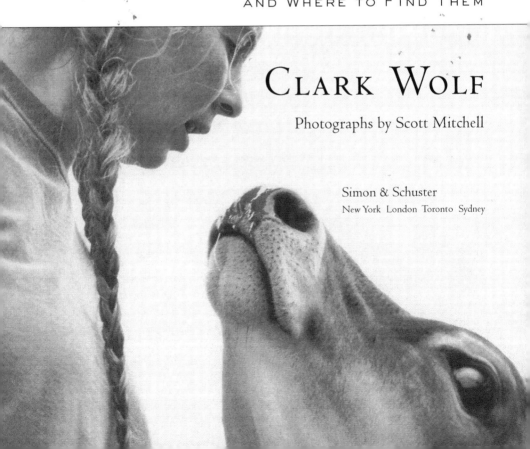

CLARK WOLF

Photographs by Scott Mitchell

Simon & Schuster
New York London Toronto Sydney

SIMON & SCHUSTER
1230 Avenue of the Americas
New York, NY 10020

First Simon & Schuster hardcover edition December 2008

SIMON & SCHUSTER and colophon are registered trademarks
of Simon & Schuster, Inc.

For information about special discounts for bulk purchases,
please contact Simon & Schuster Special Sales at
1-800-456-6798 or business@simonandschuster.com.

Designed by Joel Avirom and Jason Snyder

Manufactured in the United States of America

10 9 8 7 6 5 4 3 2 1

Library of Congress Cataloging-in-Publication Data

Wolf, Clark.
    American cheeses / Clark Wolf with photographs by Scott Mitchell.
        p.   cm.
    1. Cookery (Cheese)   2. Cheese—United States.   I. Title.
TX759.5.C48W65   2008
    641.3'73—dc22   2008017129
ISBN-13: 978-1-4516-8790-3

Acknowledgments

BOY, DID THIS BOOK TAKE A LONG TIME TO DO. I say *do* because, while not the least of it, writing was less of the effort than living, going, learning—okay, and nibbling—all while making a living from a host of other activities.

Those making this all possible were some really wonderful people who have sometimes been referred to as my assistants and associates. Really, most have been colleagues, ringmasters (Clark-sitters), and friends. They include the dear, smart, talented, and funny Caroline McDaniel; the passionate and brilliant Amanda Czepial; the magical Celina Quiros Stabel; the hilarious (sometimes even when he meant to be) and tidy Tim Shaw; Courtney Knapp; Dan Rafalin; the late heart-melting Bridgette Watkins; and the timeless, good-natured, and devoted April Sack (everyone already knows she's beautiful). And to the extraordinary Tosca Giamatti, whose dedication and patience I could not have managed without, even as she declared, "This is not as bad as I expected it to be!"—by which she meant the process of fact checking and permission getting (I hope)—I can only say biggest thanks and fondest appreciation. Now, please pass the truffles . . .

I want to especially thank Marion Cunningham. Early on, it was she who encouraged me to give this a shot, tell my stories, and not be afraid—or be afraid but do it anyway. All through this effort, she has very much been in my mind and in my heart.

I'd certainly like to thank the California Milk Advisory Board for supporting me and California cheesemakers, especially at the start of the current boom in really good dairy development out west. They also deserve credit for underwriting Dan Strongin's very good technical document, which I was happy to have at my side during the writing of this book. I also must mention the kind and generous Lynne Devereux for focusing on the best and giving so much, even on her own time, to cheesemakers and friends. Also, I do so appreciate the efforts of those who have come together to firm up and format the California Artisan Cheese Guild.

I'd like to acknowledge and thank the Wisconsin Milk Marketing Board, the Vermont Dairy Council, the New England Dairy Council, the Southern Cheese Guild, the University of Vermont, Barbara Reed at UC Davis, the American Cheese Society, and all of the other groups and institutions who have been so generous and helpful and chefs who shared their recipes.

I want to thank Roberta Klugman for helping me keep my cheese head on straight; Marian Burros for so much, including shared travels, myriad tastings, assorted recipes, and real friendship; Marion Nestle for always telling the truth about food; and Julian Armstrong for plying me with Québec's finest, and for her straightforward opinions (as if anyone could stop her).

Peggy Smith and Sue Conley deserve special thanks for sharing their time and their talents, their passion for good food and strong community, and their generosity—for being colleagues and friends on so many levels, in so many ways; Laura Chenel for her matchless talents and for being an exquisite beacon and a benchmark. The many people mentioned in this book who have worked so hard for so many years to bring along American cheesemaking also deserve all the kudos I can muster. They're the ones making the good food we're privileged to celebrate and enjoy.

I so much appreciate the support of some other pals who write, all better at this than I, who walked me through this or talked me down from the ceiling while I worked to get my rambling thoughts and scrambling brains down on paper. They include Marlena Speiler, Scott Peacock, and Kim Severson. Of course, I want to thank my editor, Sydny Miner, who believed I could—and would—do this book and who has guided me along the way.

And finally, there is no way I could have ever done this book without the precious collaboration and familial partnership of the very swell and talented Scott Mitchell. He drove the car for the first couple of years (until I hit fifty and was old enough to get my driver's license) while I mangled the directions; he never ran off the road and never punched me. And through it all he took the most heartwarming and beautiful photographs I could imagine, telling me that he was just trying to capture on film (and later digitally) what I seemed to be chatting about and exploring, reaching for

Acknowledgments

and embracing, with cheesemakers and farm animals across the country. I've told more than a few friends that I could have written some captions and gotten them published with those photos, but this has been a lot more satisfying, interesting, and fun.

Clark Wolf
New York City
September 2008

Acknowledgments

For my parents, who gave me life and the love of it

Contents

Introduction: Learning to Taste 1

What Kind of Food Is Cheese? 8

How Cheese Happens 10

Specialty, Artisan, and Farmstead Cheeses 12

How to Buy, Store, and Serve Cheese 14

The Families of Cheese 21

*How Much Is That Goat Cheese in the Window?
(or, Take Me to Your Liter)* 26

This with That: Accompaniments and Pairings 32

What the Heck Is Rennet? 34

It's a Process 35

Intolerance 36

Wrapping, Rinds, and Ripening 38

My Favorite Cheesemongers 40

Hotbeds and Bastions of Cheese Culture 43

The Northeast and New England
45

The South
107

The Middle West
147

The Wild West
183

Awards, Accolades, and Endorsements   253

Awards   254

Resources   255

Festivals   256

Metric and Other Equivalencies   257

Index   259

American
Cheeses

Introduction:
Learning to Taste

THIS IS A BOOK ABOUT CHEESE. I've wanted to write
it since about—oh—October 1980, the year I helped open the
Oakville Grocery in San Francisco. We had nearly everything
a passionate modern cook might want: free-range chickens,
organic produce, cream-top milk in bottles, hand-gathered wild
mushrooms, and fresh goat cheese lovingly handmade in Sonoma,
California, and as good as any in France, or anywhere.

I was hired as the cheese department manager. Then they
discovered I could *merchandise*. That means making things look
appealing in a way that made people grab and spend. I created
abundance to *go*.

They sent me to Manhattan to see how the big-city folks did
it: the late-lamented original Balducci's; the early, highly stylistic
Dean & DeLuca; some major Parisian players trying to conquer
the States; the ill-fated Bloomingdale's food halls. I came back
and immediately reverted to my California roots. I'd grown up

surrounded by orange groves, lemon blossoms, and watermelons piled on wooden racks (Dad would wait until they dipped to six cents a pound before he'd cave and buy). Night-blossoming jasmine and heady garden roses gave me an inkling as to how things from the earth might look and smell, even in the soon-to-be-awful San Fernando Valley. So mostly I put things in bushels and baskets. It seemed to work.

Two weeks after we unlocked the doors, I was doing all the buying and all the selling. Two months later, I was running the store. In my mid-twenties, I was really in a post-postgraduate course of all things good to eat and drink, and learning from some of the great talents in the food world.

In those months before we opened, while I was madly gathering my cheese collection, I'd also be chatting and tasting with a group that might, from time to time, include Alice Waters, Marion Cunningham, Ruth Reichl, and, of course, our boss, Joe Phelps. We're talking some major palates.

Once we got going, my learning took a slightly different course. Every week we'd take delivery of what could amount to dozens, and sometimes hundreds, of types of foods: jams, mustards, sauces, raw meat, truly frightening snacks, wild greens nobody could identify, hand-gathered wild mushrooms. But rarely did I have the offer of a new American-made cheese waiting on the tasting table.

We'd decided that fresh mozzarella was a must-have, but there was nothing in the Golden State resembling that magical *pasta filata* (pulled curd) ball I'd first seen floating in a pool of whey in the famed Formaggio Peck cheese emporium in Milan. I'll admit that the marble fountain with the carved figure of a boy spewing milky fluid up and into the carved scallop shell below may have affected my senses. But I clearly recall the nutty fragrance and tender "give" of the cheese somehow tasted of warm sunshine.

At that time I was unable to find fresh mozzarella being made out west, so I burned up the phone lines trying to have some sent from somewhere. Finally I was able to convince some poor salesperson at the Polly-O Cheese Company in Brooklyn, New York, to send me a forty-pound block of frozen cheese curd.

Up in the little apartment we'd rented as an office overlooking San Francisco on Russian Hill, we broke off bits from the massive lump of curd and dumped them into hot water. We kneaded and pulled and tried to use a wooden paddle to get a balanced, regular motion going. We achieved a sort of white rubber that bore little resemblance to mozzarella. But it taught me something. It taught me to look for benchmarks. I knew mozzarella, and this wasn't it.

Since about 1983, I've led hundreds of tastings—cheeses, oils and vinegars, wild mushrooms, herbs and spices. I always ask people what they do first when they set about to taste something new or try something they've had before, with a focus on better understanding just what it's all about. These are professionals—sometimes teachers, chefs, retailers, writers. Some say they sniff. Some poke and pull.

I say what they do—what we all do—is to quickly and unconsciously run whatever it is by our internal computer of everything we've ever tasted, loved, hated, or fantasized about eating. This visceral physical and emotional experience is universal, and it is connected to a pretty useful set of instincts, some obviously related to survival.

If a new food is vaguely reminiscent of something unhappily ingested in youth, a quick tummy turn can ensue. If it's vaguely reminiscent of a magical trip through Spain, it's something else again. And who knows what preferences we inherit at birth.

I always encourage people to be mildly aware of such reactions, while maintaining a sort of calm innocence in the experience. Don't try to be too hyperaware. Let yourself react without editing. Respond!

For most everyone who will admit it, whether or not we like a food is a quick yes or no. I like it or I don't. We can change that view and acquire a taste, but I will always find it helpful to let my body lead my mind.

For me, it was cheese that led to understanding how I could keep my palate—and my experience of food—real, a little innocent, fresh, and deeply satisfying.

———

Before I worked at the Oakville Grocery, I had opened and managed a little cheese shop at the base of Nob Hill in San

Francisco. Every day I lugged several hundred different kinds of
well-wrapped cheeses out of the walk-in refrigerator and piled
them artistically on the wooden countertop in front of two open
cases of yet more, mainly international, cheeses.

I'd been quickly trained in the world and ways of cheese shop
living, but I still needed every legend proffered by salesmen or
customers (and some I just made up or embellished) to sell those
wheels and blocks and the crackers to hold them.

I spent hours on the phone with importers and distributors
trying to separate rumor from fact, marketing from history. But if it
helped me tell the story of one cheese or another, helped me connect
a person to a specific world of taste, it was a keeper (the story), at
least until I found a better, sometimes even more authentic, tale.

I was visited every week or so by an out-of-work-Santa-looking
fellow named Jim Sebastiani, who would pull up in his little
refrigerated van and sell me too much gorgeous French cheese.
Seduced and sold, I somehow managed to get those highly perishable
treasures out the door, at a profit, in time for his next visit.

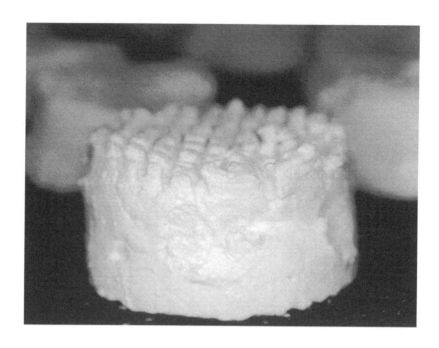

Through it all there was precious little in the way of really good American cheeses. Being in San Francisco, we sold plenty of good Jack, "fresh or dry." We'd occasionally score some wonderful four- or five-year-old Wisconsin cheddar (that the salesman claimed had been "lost in a warehouse someplace"). There was a creamy Oregon Blue, a crumbly Wisconsin Blue, and something called New York sharp. Otherwise, what we got from the United States was mostly a collection of lower-priced, lesser-quality knockoffs we cheerfully referred to as "domestic."

I still just don't much like that word. It always makes me feel as if something has been neutered or at least tamed. "Local," "regional," "American" are all more currently appealing terms, although "domestic" is literally defined as produced in or indigenous to a particular country.

In those days, "from around here" meant that it didn't have the history or the gastronomic gravitas of European foods. We were beginning to crave those goods dripping with what seemed like depth, class, charm, and quality, even then rebelling against the post-war industrially fabricated plenty of the American market basket.

Finally, just a quarter century later, we're living in a more balanced world where we can take real pride in not just how much food we crank out, but how good it is and how connected we feel to both the foods themselves and the people who make or grow them. Homegrown, artisanal cheesemakers are bringing extraordinary cheeses to market all over the country.

James Beard is known for a lot of things, but mostly he was a master teacher of home cookery who deeply valued and regularly promoted the very good foods from every corner of this country. Against his doctor's orders, I suspect he'd be pretty thrilled by what's going on in the craft of American cheesemaking. I hope you are, too.

WHAT KIND OF FOOD IS CHEESE?

Old and ancient foods seem to be all the rage these days. Heirloom fruits and vegetables, exotic spices and herbs, small-batch cheeses, of course, and whole-grain homely flatbreads all seem to be almost gaining ground against the constant onslaught of made-up and processed foods.

Dairy foods have been pilloried in the last few decades, but it was a great relief to me and anyone who loves good food when we learned that in fact butter was better for us than margarine, or any trans-fat anything.

Cheese is made from milk. That means it's high in protein and has plenty of calcium and other good stuff. It also means it has some salt and a fair amount of water. Yes, it has fat and not the best kind, but some fat is okay. Cheddar and Brie are full-fat cheeses; no cream is skimmed from the milk or added when the cheese is made. In the case of Brie, the cheese can be almost half water; cheddar contains a bit less. What that means is if a cheese is 50 percent butterfat in the solids (without water, which is the traditional way it's gauged), then it's actually about 25 percent fat. Got that? Butter is 82 to 83 percent fat. You do the math.

Let's take a quick quiz. A bite of Gouda, or a bite of Brie: which has more fat and calories? The Gouda, mostly because it has less water—unless the Brie is a double crème (60 percent fat in the solids) or triple crème (70 percent), in which case it's *still* a lower-fat and more healthful schmear than butter.

This isn't to say that cheese is diet food, but it is good, wholesome stuff that is a delicious and valuable part of most any healthy diet. Some cheeses are naturally lower in fat, like ricotta, which is made from the whey left over when another cheese is made. They've been made that way because they taste good and use what might otherwise go to waste or pig feed. But cheeses that have been traditionally made one way and are then made with lowered fat often taste a lot like chewy floor tile or quilted wrapping paper. Sorry, they just do. Same goes for low-salt. The cheese-making process just needs salt, both as an age-old natural preservative and as a natural ingredient that helps flavors develop.

I can't say this strongly enough. Eat good, natural, wholesome, and delicious cheeses in reasonable amounts and you'll be doing right by body and soul.

How Cheese Happens

Perhaps the easiest way to get a clear idea of how cheese happens is to do the following: Pour a gallon of whole milk (pasteurized or raw) into a pot and bring it to a boil. At the moment it comes to a boil, turn off the heat and pour in a quarter cup of apple cider vinegar. Now watch. What you'll see will look a whole lot like a satellite view of Hurricane Hilda as seen on the Weather Channel, but it's just a good old-fashioned separation of solids from liquid, the essential curds-and-whey experience.

Stir it around a bit with a wooden spoon, just to help move

things along. In a little while all will settle down and start to cool off. About an hour later, empty the pot into a colander lined with a double layer of cheesecloth (that you've remembered to place *in* the sink, unlike the first time I did it . . .) and let the curds drain a bit. After a few more minutes gather the corners of the cloth and tie them around that wooden spoon, then hang your new cheese bag over that same, now cooled, pot.

Put the whole thing in the fridge overnight so that it can keep draining and stay cold. In the morning, voilà! You have your own homemade fresh cheese. If you cover it with ripe berries and a fine dribble of wildflower honey, you've got breakfast or dessert. If you drizzle it with some peppery extra virgin olive oil, sprinkle on a little chopped basil and sea salt, and garnish with a few of your favorite olives, you've got a light lunch.

All cheese starts out more or less this way. Milk, heat, something to separate curds (solids) from whey (liquid), draining, and time. But at each moment early in the life of a cheese, much can change the final result: more or less heat; what's used to start the curding process; what's added to the milk (those tasty cultures) and when; what's added to the curds. Is it pressed, washed, sprayed, cooked, rubbed (sounds like a good massage!)?

I'll go into the families of cheeses and how they're related to each other in a bit, but it is important to remember that while wine has just one vintage every year, cheese has its own sort of vintage, sometimes several a day. Each critical moment of each batch of each type can create a whole different world of flavors.

Believe me, there is a lot more to making world-class cheese than I plan to go into here. This is a book for the cheese lover, not the cheesemaker. But there's much even the casual connoisseur can note that will make the experience of, as the writer Clifton Fadiman once called it, "milk's leap toward immortality" even more delicious.

SPECIALTY, ARTISAN, AND FARMSTEAD CHEESES

Most cheeses found in a shop named for things dairy and delicacy might be classified as specialties. The thing that sets specialty cheeses apart from artisan and farmstead cheeses is that the term suggests that, while special, the cheese is being made in large quantities. The French and Swiss make lots of Gruyère; the Italians roll out the Parmesan. The Dutch are long on Gouda. That doesn't mean these cheeses can't be exceedingly special.

The same is true here, which is why this book includes examples of cheddar makers and Jack mavens, mozzarella kings and blue cheese divas, who produce far too much to be included in most farmers' markets, but it's of good and consistent quality. Some things are just good.

"Artisan" means that the cheese is made according to what are sometimes called traditional methods, in what is usually a very small plant—I've seen some no larger than a twin bed—by an actual, nameable person. When it's done right, there can be a magic, an alchemy, to the process that transcends recipe. A

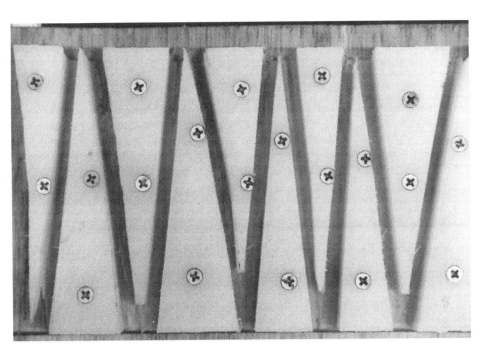

master cheesemaker can turn what seem to be simple acts of dairy cookery into a gastronomic wonder.

On the other hand, many's the capable cheesemaker who has told self-deprecatingly hilarious stories about having to feed piles and pounds of failed efforts to their dogs or pigs. (It's not just goats who will eat anything! And a good thing, too.)

In the late 1970s, Marion Cunningham, our generation's Fanny Farmer, wisely intoned that homemade bread that was lousy was, "well, dear . . . lousy bread." This from someone sufficiently impassioned about baking that she helped found the Baker's Dozen, a group of the similarly inclined who meet irregularly to share knowledge (experience, strength, and hope, if you ask me) about things baked.

Artisan cheesemaking will make more and more sense here after another couple of quick generations of consistently good and solidly profitable cheesemaking. Now it sometimes means the best intentions, and care, with regular methods and thoughtful attention, resulting in pleasant but not earth-shattering cheese.

Every year many get better and better. A recent American Cheese Society judging included more than twelve hundred entries, up hundreds from a few years before. Some greats have been around for decades—dry Jack from California, Vermont aged cheddar—but they are now being joined by a larger coterie worthy of celebration.

"Farmstead" is to cheese as "Estate Bottled" is to wine. Those winsome wheels must be made of the milk that comes from the animals right there on the farm. This guarantees some degree of charm, and often terrific stories, but by no means great cheese, though there is often a true and personal connection that results in some pretty brilliant food.

The rest is, well, something like cheese.

How to Buy, Store, and Serve Cheese

The cheese selection in the newly opened Whole Foods Market I was visiting was impressive: diverse and reasonably priced. I was finding a lot of my international and American favorites. Then I saw it: that glorious wheel of Humboldt Fog, among the best goat tommes to come along in generations, was mangled beyond repair.

Some enthusiastic but untrained clerkazoid had been maniacally hacking wedges from the whole round cheese. Not a good sign.

A wheel of cheese should always be cut in half, then wrapped. Wedges should be cut from one or the other of those halves. If what I've described above is in evidence at your local cheese counter, you just might be in the wrong shop.

In fact, it's an issue that has always been central to buying good cheese. We've nearly lost touch with any real sense of the butcher and the baker (and when it comes to candle makers, I prefer the French Diptyque). But a growing number of devoted cheesemongers are plying their reborn and updated trade in good shops across the country. Failing one of these new dairy masters, a friendly clerk or department manager with a regular schedule is the safest bet. Otherwise, I'm never too shy about telling whoever is manning the knife just how I want my piece cut.

The way a cheese, or any food, looks has a lot to do with my decision about whether or not to toss it into the shopping basket. Some of it is learned. A lot of us have gotten over the need to pick what looks like picture-perfect fruits and vegetables, realizing that sometimes, say, an apple bred for visual perfection can taste a lot like packing material. We've come to know that a bruise here, a funny stripe there, an odd shape, or a varied coloration can, for the right variety, mean peak seasonal bliss.

So, too, with cheese. Sometimes the moldy, aged smelly slime on the outside suggests creamy wonder within.

But mostly, it is good if it looks good. And if it looks like

fermented roadkill, it might be best to ask a few questions and inquire about trying a little taste.

There's often a much wider range of what's called "right" with a cheese for most people. One favorite example is something the French call *frais du sel*, or "fresh from the salt." The milk gets turned to curds and formed into a flattened round, maybe even inoculated with the spores that are meant to become a fluffy white coat of soft-ripening mold. But after just a quick dip in a salty bath, the cheese is chilled and shipped, and happily scarfed as a gentle, tasty fresh cheese. Marin French Cheese in Petaluma, California, makes their own version of this cheese and calls it Breakfast Cheese.

In other cases, the younger cheese does in fact—as the Brie would if properly handled—become something entirely different and wonderful in its own way. Young Gouda with time can become a sweet, hard, pleasantly grainy and grindable wonder.

Which brings us to storing cheese. This is so different from the fairly delicate, and at times rigorous, task of ripening cheese, the process that the French call *affinage*. The word means to bring a living cheese along just so, until it can achieve a time-honored, historically evolved state of agreed-upon perfection. Usually this was to fit the taste of the king (or queen) or other wealthy patrons. Later on it became the purview of a discerning, often contentious cognoscenti. In Italy, similar sorts of cheese might be made in town after town, with just a slight variation that gave each village its own cause to boast. Many of the best American cheeses echo European cousins. Others have their own evolving flavors. The benchmarks they set are, in many cases, just being recognized.

In the 1970s, when I got acquainted with some of the better cheeses of the world, the magic that kept cheese fresh was plastic wrap. Stored in long, heavy boxes with lethal serrated cutting edges at the opening, we pulled and folded, stretched and tucked, and made the so-called face of each cheese look glassed. It made for an impressive display.

At home, I was committed to the same process with purloined stretch-wrap. For a while I tried Tupperware, then resealable plastic bags. I felt too modern to wrap my cheese in a slightly brine-moistened towel and stash it at the lower back of my fridge, as I'd heard from foodie friends in the 1960s.

Then one day I found some old-fashioned waxed paper sandwich bags in a whole foods (small w) store and tried one on a wedge. A few days later I noted an artisan cheesemaker using only waxed paper on her treasured $24-a-pound tomme and felt I was onto something. These days I find that slightly waxed butcher paper does the trick. In fact, I prefer it to plastic wrap, which seems to encourage the growth of undesirable mold.

Fresh rewraps are certainly a good thing, but what I do find to be the only two universally helpful rules are: (1) Keep all the cheese in one drawer in the fridge (we'll talk rotation and ripening in a moment) and (2) scrape off any mold or other dry and nasty bits before serving.

Serving cheese really shouldn't have to be a big deal. To begin with, most cheeses are so beautiful in their natural states that little embellishment is really necessary. As long as we all stop hacking good cheese into sad little cubes, we can pretty much enjoy whatever wonderful cheese strikes our fancy.

One perfect cheese is a good way to go. Try for something your guests will recognize and something that looks familiar but is a little special. Serve it at room temperature with crunchy accompaniments—apples, pears, walnuts, dried fruit, fairly simple crackers, and grapes—always, if you can, grapes.

Another time, set out three cheeses of various types and styles. Something creamy and rich, something salty and deep, and something goat. Then move on to five—maybe adding a blue, a peppery sheep's milk cheese, and a stinky washed-rind something.

Don't try to be too clever. This isn't a challenge for you or your guests. It's supposed to be a pleasure.

THE FAMILIES OF CHEESE

I don't know about you, but I've been lucky to have sweet parents and close cousins, a sibling, some aunts and uncles. I even remember my grandparents, and at least one great-grandie. What has that got to do with cheese? Well, many cheeses, while unique and special, are related. You can learn a lot about one from knowing another. They share similar traits and spark familiar responses.

Sometimes the child (a soft or fresh cheese) becomes an adult version (a mature cheese) of its early incarnation. Sometimes what happens later on seems a total transformation.

Let's look at what has traditionally been thought of as the families of cheese, with my personal observations.

The list often goes like this:

Fresh

Soft and soft-ripened

Semi-soft

Semi-firm and firm

Hard

Blue

Goat

Sheep

But sometimes fresh varieties like Crescenza or even Brie and some goat cheeses can become soft or soft-ripened, and age successfully even on to dry, hard, grateable cheeses. Sometimes a semi-soft table cheese, like a young Gouda, can evolve, with time achieving what might be considered nearly nine lives. A blue can also be soft-ripened, as can goat or sheep's milk cheese.

After running that little cheese shop in San Francisco for a couple of exhausting years, I took myself to Europe to broaden my education and have some international fun. I got to the wholesale food market just outside of Paris at a place called Rungis. There my eyes went wide as I ambled into and through two airplane hangar–sized buildings filled with cheeses from everywhere imaginable.

I may not have known the story or recipes of every one. I may not have been able to recite the cheesemaker's name or the perfect wine pairing for every crateful, but I found I knew, basically, what everything was. This was fresh goat. That looked to be soft-ripened and wrapped in an earthy leaf. Another looked aged and hard as stone and smelled sweet.

The point is, if you can get comfortable with understanding the nature of how something gets made, and how its basic ingredients and handling might affect it, you can approach almost any cheese with a startling degree of recognition.

What I hope you'll take from this book is a more-than-basic feel for cheese that will help and let you explore, experiment, and, most important, enjoy a growing world of wonderfully made American cheeses. (And you can try some of that international stuff, too, if you like.)

You'll need to treat **fresh** cheese like any other fresh dairy food. Keep it cold and eat it up soon. There are exceptions to the "eat it soon" rule like Brie and Crescenza or others that have been made to eat fresh but will ripen nicely if kept around, but these cheeses still need to be refrigerated.

Soft and **soft-ripened** cheeses need to be kept cool and enjoyed when they're ripe and ready to go. Let your shopkeeper do the major ripening, but if the cheese is close to edible or if you want to buy it ahead to prepare for next weekend's party, take it out and keep it (wrapped) in a cool part of the kitchen for an hour or so a day, until it gives at the touch. Just remember to flip it once a day so that the cheese doesn't settle to the bottom while the water floats out the top. If it's a spray-mold cheese like Brie, check for that cat-box—okay, secondary fermentation—stinky ammoniated smell.

You'll know the smell if it hits you. If it does, first try leaving the cheese out, unwrapped, for a while. Sometimes it's just on the surface and wrapping. If it's still there, cut into the cheese and sniff and taste the inside. If it hasn't yet invaded the interior, there may be hope. You can cut off the entire rind and serve the cheese (soon) or even roll the soft, now rindless cheese in herbs or chopped nuts. Maybe toss bread crumb—coated pieces into a hot pan of seasoned olive oil and create tasty hors d'oeuvres or what I like to call "surprise croutons" that ooze molten whatever when you cut or bite into them. The key is to not totally panic when a little nasty stink reaches for your nose.

Semi-soft cheeses are the easiest to deal with, on a lot of levels. They're often mild and a great introduction to cheese loving for a lot of folks (kids included). They require little care and only need loose wrapping to keep moisture in, especially after they're cut.

They do, however, like all cheeses, manage to take on smells and tastes from other foods around them. Ever leave a partially unwrapped stick of butter in the fridge overnight? The next day it somehow tastes of old Chinese food and potato salad. It's fat and water, mostly, two things that take on tastes and smells rather well. That's why I suggested before that cheeses all be kept in one drawer or one covered tub in the fridge.

The good news is that if what's in and around your cheese— herbs, spices, a brine- or wine-soaked rind, a fig or chestnut leaf, some mushroomy, well-chosen mold—has some complementary tastiness, then all will be better than well. If the only other foods nearby are other cheeses, of any family, then these are developments that can actually turn to gastronomic treasure.

However, except for the occasional traveling blue mold (which really takes a while to develop and might not be so bad anyway), unintentional mold is not usually a plus. Remove it completely, but unless it's pink (which can indicate some bad stuff), don't worry.

Care of **semi-firm** and **firm** cheeses is similar to that for semi-softies, except that like some fine wines, these cheeses are built to age well and slowly, and last a long time. For very **hard** cheeses, some people like to wrap them loosely in a damp towel or cheesecloth and let them continue to dry. It's an old-fashioned method, but it works.

The same storage methods hold true, with some minor variations, for all cow, goat, or sheep's milk cheese.

How Much Is That Goat Cheese in the Window? (or, Take Me to Your Liter)

I was on the phone with a friend when she mentioned her shock at the cost of a few ounces of a new regional cheese from a couple of counties north. It was $18. Not for a pound, but for what seemed to be a six-ounce piece of perfectly nice, locally made artisan cheese.

Why does really good cheese seem to cost so much? Let's start with the milk. Cows give about eight gallons a day, sometimes more, usually year-round or at least most of a good year. Unless the herd is pedigreed (some people love the higher fat content of Jersey milk, for example), milk in most parts of the country is considered a commodity and sells at sometimes painfully low prices. That's why some dairy farmers have turned to cheesemaking, to actually get the added value of time, talent, and taste that comes from the milk their animals produce.

Goats give the equivalent of about three tall bottles of imported mineral water daily, that is, about three liters, or a little less than three quarts. In some climates and conditions, herds can be managed to give milk much of the year, but as a cheesemaker friend said not long ago, "Animals give milk for their young, not for us." Goats are usually friendly animals and fairly easy to raise, but they don't produce popular wool, and their meat is only just starting to become more widely accepted, so there's not that much goat's milk to go around.

And then there's sheep. I learned a bit about sheep on a visit with a friend to northern Illinois. We found ourselves on a dark country road when suddenly our headlights illuminated scores of what looked to be little green glowing orbs. What luck, I thought. Here the city boy makes his first trip to the countryside and the Martians invade.

After a few moments we adjusted to the darkness and my friend informed me that these were, in fact, just the reflective eyes of a large and languid herd of sheep. I honked the horn, revved the engine, and even yelled like a New York cabdriver for them to move their woolly

selves. Nothing I did garnered more than a puzzled glance. Finally, my friend Alice gently informed me that if we were to get back to her family's farm before the sun rose, one of us (me) was going to have to do a little sheep shoving.

I positioned myself, as instructed, behind one big girl who actually seemed to notice my presence, and pushed. She slowly got to her feet, looked at me wide-eyed and sideways, and began to move forward, toward a point off and across the road. The others, being sheep, slowly got up—as if to say "Oh, we're going for a walk now"—and followed that first girl out of our way.

All of this to say that sheep act like, well, sheep. If there's a storm a-comin' or one of the flock feels blue or there's a new horse in the corral or a new dog in the field, they may just get freaked out and decide not to give milk, or be too upset to move easily into the milking barn. And when all is well, they still give only about a liter a day per sheep.

———

Really good handcrafted cheeses can be expensive. I think of cheese at three or four price levels and try to make sure I feel comfortable with what I'm getting when I buy each kind.

The lowest-priced category is large-production cheese, sometimes called grocery store cheese. In a pinch, I'll go there, especially when I'm on a budget or making a dish that calls for melted cheese.

Then there's specialty cheese. To me, this is larger-production cheese with a memorable style and good, solid quality. Remembering that some "art films" can be dull, painful, and, well, just bad art, so, too, can some cheeses striving to be special end up simply wrong. I will never love pesto cheese, cheese with chocolate, or cheese blended with smoked salmon. Granted, there is history (Sage Derby from England or Dutch Leyden) for folding pepper, herbs, or spices into cheese curds now and then to create a classic. If not for jalapeño Jack, that pleasant table cheese from Monterey, California, and the flavors of the Southwest might never have gone mainstream.

Then there are the third and fourth tiers: artisan (small batch, handcrafted) and farmstead, really a subset of artisan cheese. They really do deserve to get a higher price than those listed above.

But again, it's all about what you personally value. Many's the time I've sported for a pricey handmade cheese that turned out to be only okay, but I was glad to support the cause and encourage the evolution of the craft. More often when I splurge, it's because I know and love a brilliantly made American cheese and am thrilled to luxuriate in something handcrafted with passion and care, often by someone I've read about or even someone I know and admire.

I have great respect for the people who spend hours and years exploring the nuances of wines and matching every wine—or these days, even micro-brewed beer or cider—with its perfect cheese, and the other way round, too. I'm just not one of those people.

I prefer to start with the simpler foods that go with almost any cheese, and move on from there. Flatbreads, walnuts, dried fruits. You can't go wrong.

I'm happy with a ripe—or even crisp—pear, an heirloom apple (when's the last time you had an in-season, unwaxed, organic Red Delicious apple? Yes, Red Delicious!), and most kinds of grapes. With fresh cheeses, if they have a little tartness going on, I love sliced tomatoes and cracked pepper, ripe avocado, a drizzle of olive oil, and a leaf of nearly any tasty green.

As to wine, let's face it: most cheese enjoyed in restaurants goes happily with whatever's left over from the meal, or one more glass of something else recommended by the waiter. The end of a long, happy evening is not a time to struggle with deep thinking and big choices.

That said, there are some lovely basics to consider, and plenty of discoveries to share. In fact, many's the cheese that has made a middling wine come to life. Who knew that oaky chardonnay went wonderfully with sharp cheddar? Fermented with fermented just works.

The practice has great logic: historically, people enjoyed the local wines with the local cheeses. In his very good book *A Wine Journey along the Russian River*, Steve Heimoff talks about terroir as more than just the dirt. It really can be thought of as a sort of local sensibility about flavors and styles that emerges over time in a region. As our wine and our cheese regions grow and develop, this will certainly be useful thinking. But I find that, without getting too specific, I have most success going *along with* or *up against* flavors. That is, I may choose a wine that's as zippy or as creamy as my cheese, or I may try one that contrasts with the prevailing or dominant characters.

But as a recent study at the University of California at Davis stated, the stronger the cheese, the more it dulls the palate and so overpowers any real experience of some of the subtler, perhaps even more desirable, flavors of a red wine. It's just good sense that a full-fat cheese, with its own pack of fermented flavors, might be too much for that hint of anise, that whiff of spring flowers and wild berries, about which wine writers wax poetic.

When I eat something at the beginning of an evening, I'm careful not to fill myself up or so coat my palate that only a shot of vinegar on the rocks would clear things out sufficiently to register what comes next. Even when I exercise the very American habit of slathering some butter on good bread—something lovely from Vermont Butter & Cheese or Straus Family Creamery—I always sprinkle on a little salt. First, because I love salt and, second, to keep my taste buds in the game.

When I have a truly great bottle of rare wine to enjoy, I try to make sure that at least some of it is quaffed without competition, on its own, for some singular moments of glory. Then on to the cheese!

What the Heck Is Rennet?

I've described the simplest way to imagine the "make"—when milk gets turned to cheese. Now let's chat a bit about some of the key elements.

Rennet is the classic starter that helps turn the milk into those proverbial curds and whey. Originally it came from enzymes found in the stomach lining of a suckling animal. It makes sense. When a critter's very young, it needs special help breaking down nourishment and somehow, legends aside (see below), folks learned to harness that process and make cheese.

If you're not familiar with the story, it's said that a Bedouin kept his lunch of fresh milk in a bladder made from the stomach of a newly slaughtered calf. Much work and travel caused our hero to forget his nourishment until the next day. When he opened the pouch, what remained was fresh curd cheese. The fellow tried it, and the rest, as they say, is cheese history.

But forgetful herdsmen aside, animal rennet is not the only starter made popular over centuries of experimentation. The Romans used select thistles, and the bits of stem that hold fig to tree seemed to work well, too.

These days there are certainly a host of choices; cheesemakers use either animal rennet or what they call vegetable rennet, a natural complex of enzymes. Obviously, vegetarians and kosher-keeping folks prefer the latter. Cheesemakers choose what seems best for what they're trying to achieve, and they don't mind being asked which they're using for any particular tomme.

It's a Process

I'm a little embarrassed to admit it, but for the longest time I
thought it was called "processed" cheese, as in *finished* through
some secret method and now *done*. Actually, process cheese is
usually a reworking of less-than-stellar cheese with the addition of
milk, whey, salt, some vegetable gums, flavorings, stabilizers, and
preservatives into a useful, stable food source that can be adjusted
to suit the palate of a broad audience and be achieved at low costs.
Process cheese is sometimes blasted from a can or hacked from
a gelatinous block or formed into iconic squares and wrapped in
sheets of plastic and called American cheese. But it actually isn't
cheese.

I try never to eat any.

There is, however, a long history of what I can only call re-
worked cheese. Remember fondue? It's melted cheese, a little
booze, and some seasoning. Then there's raclette, which came from
an Alpine tradition of putting the wheel of cheese close to the
fireplace to melt the surface, the better to serve it with a crust of
bread, a roasted potato, or a hunk of onion.

Many of the other cheeses you see flecked with peppers or
pesto are actually fully natural cheese, with the herbs or spices
gently folded into freshly formed curds, then pressed into wheels
or blocks for more classical aging.

Intolerance

I hate intolerance of almost any sort, but lactose intolerance makes me sad. Fresh milk is full of lactose, or milk sugar. Fresh cheese may have some, but most aged cheeses that have been around for sixty days or more have virtually none of those milk sugars the feisty bacteria that cause gastrointestinal distress find so tasty.

This is one reason that cheeses from other countries don't get to come here until they've been around for two months: because that point when most of the lactose has been gobbled up is also when most experts agree any of the undesirable or possibly dangerous bacteria that might be in the cheese have all died off as well. This is the simplest way I know to explain why aged raw milk cheeses are flavorful but more than safe to eat.

There continues to be a lot of discussion about the safety of raw milk cheese. Cheesemaker Mariano Gonzalez—these days crafting bandage-wrapped cheddar and San Joaquin Gold for Fiscallini in Modesto, California—grew up in Uruguay. For him, milk is always raw—so much so that he claims a guaranteed tummy ache if he's forced to drink the wholesome, pasteurized, homogenized style of American childhood we call regular milk. Mariano, along with a growing number of Americans, is passionate about the magical nature of raw milk, for drinking and for cheesemaking. There's no doubt that raw milk cheesemakers have more flavor components to work with. There are simply more little cultures in there.

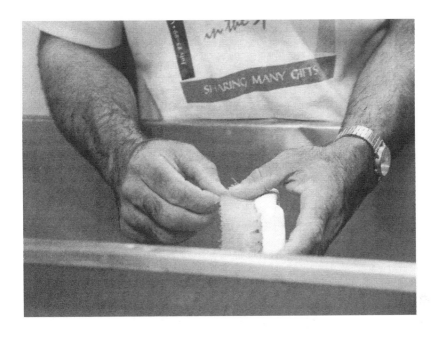

There are a lot of romantic notions associated with fresh milk untouched by modern science and technology. Many cheesemakers feel strongly that they have a much better chance of producing great cheese if the milk is raw. That can certainly be true. But in fact, one cheesemaker I know feels that using unpasteurized milk is almost like cheating; it feels to her as if she's relinquishing some of the craft, maybe even some of the art of her work, and in fact her cheeses are extraordinary, and from carefully pasteurized milks.

But there are good reasons for and wonderful results from many methods associated with insisting that milk is pure and wholesome for cheesemaking. They include how the animals are kept and cared for; how far the milk travels and by what means it gets to where it's to become cheese; and, if and how it's pasteurized, if, as I call them, the gentle, regular, or super-charged (really high-test, which tries to kill everything, including much of the taste) method is used.

Each method has its proponents and its place, and all should be considered, depending on the situation.

WRAPPING, RINDS, AND RIPENING

"Am I supposed to eat this part?" is a question I've been asked countless times over the years. My answer varies.

If it's a hard washed rind, then it depends on your taste (it can be a good flavoring in soup) and how old and stinky it is. If it's a spray mold, the white and fluffy coating on the outside of an award-winning soft-ripened triple crème, well, why not? I think of those ripened mold spores as tiny wild mushrooms. If it's wax—well, no, unless you're trying to make those big red lips. Wax of any sort (preferably over a bandage wrapping) is there to prevent the wrong sorts of stuff from growing, to keep moisture in, and to let the little universe of that particular cheese develop in peace. Leaves such as chestnut or grape may impart a certain herbaceousness, but mostly they're for pleasing show, and for that moisture retention thing. Natural vegetable ash is usually found on the outside of various goat cheeses and sometimes patted between layers of curd before the cheese gets finished. It may add a bit to taste and texture, may do the charcoal filter thing with the ripening cheese, and may create a slight barrier to the growing of unwanted mold, but the big deal is in the looks.

Most cheese ripens from the outside in. That is why you might get a creamy thing going on out near the rind but find things firm at the center. It's more pronounced with soft cheeses but shows up with semi-soft and even firmer ones.

Blue cheeses do the opposite. They're inoculated with spores (that go blue or a tasteful blue-gray or blue-green eventually) and are poked full of holes so air can get in and help get things going. The French refer to the look of a fully ripened blue cheese as "parsleyed," like that decorative garnish green (actually, I love chopped parsley with dry Jack and a little olive oil . . . but I digress).

Don't panic if you see a favorite cheese all sealed up in some plastic vacuum pack. Although it may present a challenge to the

pleasant development of a nice rind, it's often done to hold in that precious moisture while the cheese is being shipped across great expanses of the countryside or stored in large warehouses. It doesn't mean that ripening has stopped, because cheese ripens anaerobically (which means in a vacuum) and so all may eventually go as desired once the wheel is unpacked and left to finish aging.

And finally, yes, it's just fine to eat the outside rind of most any soft-ripened and even lightly ash-coated cheese. I love it, if it's not too ripe. And how do you tell when things have gone too far? It's that window-cleaner-meets-cat-box moment. So cut off the outside and see if the inside is still simply tangy and earthy. And enjoy it just the way *you* like to eat your cheese.

My Favorite Cheesemongers

Cheesemonger is the traditional title for those folks who select, gather, ripen, display, and disperse a whole world of dairy goods.

My first experience with these intense counter jockeys was in Berkeley, California, at the Co-Op Cheese Board. It wasn't until I moved to New York City in 1982 that I started to meet some world-class tasting buds, colleagues, and cheese pals.

What is it about Manhattan that makes cheese folks cranky? Ed Edelman, well-respected original owner of the Ideal Cheese Shop and coauthor with Susan Grodnik of *The Ideal Cheese Book*, was a legendary curmudgeon. Steve Jenkins, star of the expansive Upper West Side Fairway Market and author of the very good book *Cheese Primer*, is almost always up for a blood pressure–raising philosophical tussle. Giorgio DeLuca of the once trendsetting, stylish Dean & DeLuca shops has been known to charm the leaves off trees, then snap a twig or two; and this generation's owner of Greenwich Village's former discount dairy store Murray's Cheese, Rob Kaufelt—well, let's just say that I'm thrilled that he's such an energetic promoter of American-made cheeses and leave it at that.

Then there's the distinctly New York culture and style tempered with midwestern warmth and charm of Ari Weinzweig of the always deeply satisfying Zingerman's Deli in Ann Arbor, Michigan. Here's a guy who travels the world and brings it home for the folks, while displaying a generosity of time and spirit, and a palate every bit as sharp as those Manhattan hotshots.

Ihsan Gurdal of Formaggio Kitchen in Cambridge, Massachusetts, has brought Europe a little closer in the cellar under his shop and spawned quite a few junior cheese mavens, now well on to their own successes.

And more recently, in Manhattan, Max McCalman of Artisanal and Picholine and author of the lovely books *The Cheese Plate* and *Cheese: A Connoisseur's Guide to the World's Best* has warmed up to non-European cheeses and brought his depth and passion to the topic.

In Southern California I have enjoyed stopping in to visit the counter at La Brea Bakery in Santa Monica, where Nancy Silverton and her crew oversee glorious baked goods and a heck of a cheese collection, including some very local and national varieties seen few other places. I also admire the Beverly Hills Cheese Shop, the

Introduction: Learning to Taste

Cheese Shop of Carmel, and the Pasta Shop up north in Oakland and Berkeley. But it is two women, both from the Washington, D.C., area who have built a new legacy and, more than any others, lead the way.

I met Peggy Smith when she was a cook at Chez Panisse, and Sue Conley after she had helped open Bette's Oceanview Diner in Berkeley, California, where she was just getting focused on American cheesemaking. These are the gals who do it all. They make fresh, soft-ripened, and aged cheeses. They select, ripen, and ship some of the world's best, and they do all this while being enormously generous in so many related and unrelated areas that it's too much to list. They are largely responsible for cheeses from Neal's Yard Dairy and from many young graduates of those London masters now so much a part of our national cheese network and culture. Their Cowgirl Creamery is located at Tomales Bay Foods in the lovely Point Reyes Station of the pastoral region of the northern San Francisco Bay Area, with a sister shop at the landmark Ferry Building in San Francisco and another back in D.C.; they are as much as any other shop responsible for America's discovery of major homegrown talent.

Hotbeds and Bastions
of Cheese Culture

What is it about college towns that makes for good cheese? Is it all that education going on? Master's degree candidates willing to work for hourly wages if there's a chance for good storytelling and cultural exchange?

In the last thirty years the best cheese towns seem to have been Berkeley, California; Ann Arbor, Michigan; Austin, Texas; Burlington, Vermont; and maybe Cambridge, Massachusetts.

Then there's New York and San Francisco. Big cities with plenty of restaurants, they are the first couple of locales where knowing a lot about cheese can actually get you a good job in a handsome restaurant.

But no matter the town, really good cheeses sometimes come and go. Some are seasonal—well, really, the milk is—and some are made in small enough batches to simply run out or become quickly scarce. Like peaches in summer, good cheese is worth waiting for.

Whether it's Star Provisions in Atlanta or Pastoral in Chicago, one of the big boys in New York or the Cowgirls in San Francisco, trust your dedicated cheese shopkeeper to be well supplied with what's good, right now. If you fall in love with something special, let them know and get yourself on a list, old-fashioned phone or e-mail. I used to pull out a tattered, hand-written phone list when the Mozzarella di Bufala Campana arrived in an E-container from the now defunct Eastern Airlines. Our three dozen faithful showed up at the San Francisco Oakville Grocery within hours—and loaded up on vine-ripened tomatoes, paper-thin sliced prosciutto, and fragrant charante melons.

Now the mozzarella is made in this country from the milk of all-American water buffalo and even the prosciutto is locally cured. With any luck, this will convince us all that it's okay to wait until some spring cheeses are ready in the fall, some winter milk wonders just perfect for a summer's night.

The Northeast and New England

WE TOOK THE RED-EYE TO NEW YORK to spend
Christmas day with James Beard. Brunch was simple, as were all
his meals, but striking. A Smithfield ham set on a long board at
the kitchen island. The salty ham was served with shiny, sticky, and
spicy mustard fruits. Salt, sugar, pork. A revelation.

A duo of purees—vivid red beets and deep green spinach—
gave a nod to the holidays. There was a joint of beef, Welsh rarebit,
and brussels sprouts. The nine-year-old mincemeat came from a
crock in the corner on the floor. Generous portions were covered
with hard sauce and swallowed down with plenty of port.

The next day we made the food shop rounds: Dean & DeLuca,
Balducci's, Zabars. It was 1981 and fancy foods (or "gore-mee
foods," as James called them) were becoming all the rage. There,
with my friend John Carroll, Beard's West Coast assistant, at my
side, we rambled around the specialty foods world of Manhattan
for that long, cold, magical weekend. New York was, and is, more

a crossroads and showcase for really good food than an original source. (I've often said that if it grows in Manhattan, scrape it off.) I was a fledgling cheesemonger in search of raw milk wonders. So we set off to sample the best the world had to offer.

James sent me off to Ideal Cheese, and Ed Edelman, who was the prototypical Manhattan cheesemonger. Grumpy, aloof, opinionated, and just plain cranky, this accomplished curmudgeon seemed to actually discourage commerce in his tiny, well-stocked shop. I asked about American cheeses. He said there were few worth mentioning. He gave me a taste of a sharp and creamy Vermont cheddar, then tried to move me to Canadian Oka or something French.

The Northeast hotbed of regional cheese life is arguably Burlington, Vermont. Take a late afternoon flight from Boston or New York in time to slip into Smokejacks, a cozy spot just off the town square. There, a sort of Berkeley-friendly-funky-meets-domestic-partner bistro offers one of the best local and occasional international cheese selections I've found.

The English influence on New England cheesemaking has finally abated somewhat. Yes, there's plenty of good cheddar. And Colby, or more accurately Crowley, perhaps the oldest continuously made cheese in the States. A washed-curd cousin of cheddar, it's clean, almost squeaky, and wonderfully homely. At its best, it's transcendentally plain, in the best sense of the word. This, at a time when knowledgeable Americans are finally beginning to realize the values and sophistication of brilliant simplicity.

It seems that almost every week there is a new cheese from Vermont or Maine or Massachusetts coming to market, building on a history of cheese production in the region that brought us our first cheese factory (in Rome, New York, in 1851), many cooperatives (like the 1919 formation of Cabot Creamery in an 1893-built dairy), and quite a few classics (like the Herkimer Cheese Company, since 1949).

While most of the early well-known cheeses in New England were made from cow's milk, truth be told, if there was in fact any cheese at the first Thanksgiving in 1621, it was probably goaty and fresh. The early English settlers certainly brought these adaptable, versatile, and fairly low-maintenance (and friendly) animals along for what would become quite an amazing adventure.

PROFILE:

Frank Kosikowski

No book on modern American cheesemaking would be complete without a few words in praise of the pioneering efforts of a man many knew simply as Dr. Frank or Kos. In fact there's an award at Cornell University called the Kos Award, named for him.

Frank Kosikowski's benchmark book, *Cheese and Fermented Milk Foods*, while less than romantic in title, has long been what might be called the Old Testament of twentieth-century cheesemaking since it was first published in 1966. Now in its third edition, the two-volume set is still very much part of the current explosion of the kind of artisan and farmstead cheesemaking he championed.

This is the guy who may have turned the word "mentor" into a verb. His disciples include academics, scientists, artisans, and the sorts of passionate professionals who even now are leapfrogging backward, with the most modern approaches to some of the most ancient methods of turning milk into longer-lasting and deeply satisfying foods.

Paul Kindstedt's *American Farmstead Cheese* is, by its own assessment, "The Complete Guide to Making and Selling Artisan Cheese." Its author credits Dr. Frank with being his teacher and inspiration. Kosikowski is renowned for many significant accomplishments, not the least of which was the formation of today's quite influential American Cheese Society. He was a visionary and a heck of a teacher.

CHEESEMAKER:

John and Janine Putnam
Thistle Hill Farm

There are several sorts of cheesemakers working today. First, there is the classic cheese- and dairy-making family, handing down traditions from one generation to the next, sometimes skipping generations. Then there are the back-to-the-landers, mostly from the 1960s and '70s, who felt working a farm to be an important political choice. Some have evolved to be among the most critically acclaimed artisans, proving that good intentions and good taste can indeed go together. There are certainly some of what they used to call "gentlemen farmers" who like the idea of having freshly made cheeses handcrafted on their manicured lands.

But there is also a newer breed of cheesemaker who may be on a second (or third) career or just starting out in life, but who has made a serious decision to make a life and a business crafting special cheeses and bringing them to market.

The folks at Thistle Hill Farm fall into this hardworking group. John and Janine Putnam in North Pomfret, Vermont, made a plan, built a farm, mastered cheesemaking, and now give us a first-class Alpine-style wheel called Tarentaise. It tastes of wine and sweet grasses and, like its cousins the Gruyères, raclettes, and appenzellers of Switzerland and France, is lovely for melting into or onto all sorts of warming dishes.

Thistle Hill Farm

PO Box 255

North Pomfret, VT 05053

Tel.: 802-457-9349

www.ThistleHillFarm.com

info@thistlehillfarm.com

CHEESE:

Organic Tarentaise

CHEESEMAKER:

Annette Meriweather
Menhennett Farms

It's not easy to get a taste of Annette Meriweather's very good
sheep's milk cheeses. They're made and aged to be ready for sale
the first week in May, at the Maryland Sheep and Wool Festival in
West Friendship, near Baltimore, Maryland, and they always sell
out—last year, in less than three hours!

A classic herd of pure Shropshire ewes gives rich milk
that goes into her blue-veined cheeses: Steelton, named for the
favorite English blue and for a real place called Steelville nearby;
and an American Shropshire blue, similar to the English variety,
as well as some fresh cheeses and a hand-formed Greek-style
round called Metsovo (smoked and plain). But the blues are the
ones worth a trip.

The day we visited this classic farm in Amish country, we
stood with Annette and her head cheesemaker, Lee Cook, by the
flock, when suddenly, almost quietly, we felt a low rumble. Like
a painting come to life, we saw a young man, probably still in
his teens, gently guiding an old wooden hay wagon, pulled by a
huge long-haired horse. He seemed to be floating through the
long stand of trees that bordered the farm. The moment was a
melding of past and present, time and place, like stepping into
an old film.

Menhennett Farms

1688 Bryson Road

Cochranville, PA 19330

Tel.: 610-593-5726

CHEESES:

Steelton

Metsovo

American Shropshire Blue

Fromage Bleu

Ricki Carroll
New England Cheesemaking Supply Company

In the beginning there was Ricki. Well, maybe not on the *Mayflower*, but since the start of this generation's current cheese boom in the 1970s, Ricki Carroll has been teaching people about the universal basics of cheesemaking.

It all started with a couple of goats, the second bought to keep the first one company (and quiet). She had to learn to milk to keep them happy, which led to some experimenting with home cheesemaking. That ended up making her, and her then husband, Bob, popular with friends.

Before taking off for England on the educational journey that would change her life, she thought about getting good prices on equipment she might later need and decided to see if freelancing as an equipment wholesaler might lead to some additional income. She placed a $9 ad in the *Dairy Goat Journal*. "Want to make cheese?" it said. "Send 25 cents for a catalogue."

On her return from England, Ricki found the mailbox stuffed with quarters. She knew that this meant there was a market out there clamoring for cheesecloth, presses, kits, rennet, cultures, and knowledge.

In 1978 her early workshops were priced at $20 for a full day, including a meal from her organic garden, with homemade dandelion wine. It seemed that there were always a fresh half-dozen eager students ready to fill up her weekend days.

By 1982 she had published her first edition of *Cheesemaking Made Easy*, which was revised in 1996 and again in 2002, when it was rechristened *Home Cheesemaking*. Many's the successful cheesemaker or monger who learned at the knee of Ricki Carroll: the wonderful women at Orb Weaver in Vermont, the folks at Coach Farms in New York, and the master of the legendary Zingerman's Deli in Ann Arbor, Michigan, among them.

What Ricki taught, and shares to this day, that has made the most significant impact is a basic sensibility about how a number of classic cheeses might be created, might ripen, taste, and be enjoyed. New England Cheesemaking is still the go-to place for fledgling and passionate cheese folk.

New England Cheesemaking Supply Company
PO Box 85
Ashfield, MA 01330
Tel.: 413-628-3808
Fax: 413-628-4061
www.cheesemaking.com
info@cheesemaking.com

Dawn Morin-Boucher
Green Mountain Blue Cheese

We were looking for a 1,200-acre farm that had once been part of a General Champlain land grant to a farmer growing food to feed the massing troops during the American Revolution. We almost went too far and ended up in Canada.

In the middle of this northern Vermont splendor we found Dawn Morin-Boucher, her husband, Dan, and his brother Denis's family, working the land.

Like so many other farming families, Dan and Denis's parents wanted to retire from active work and pass along the property for the next generation. This meant that the spread had to support three families instead of one. It meant that as a milk-only dairy farm they would have to produce some three million gallons of milk a year. At first, Dawn tried to help the farm be totally self-sufficient, growing all their food and making every stitch they wore, but she soon found it daunting. "It's a full-time job not to work." Now that brother-in-law Denis handles the land, husband Dan looks after the cows, and Dawn turns the result into award-winning cheese, total milk production

needs only to hit the million-gallon mark to pay the bills. They even have the occasional day off.

Dawn started out like so many others, with myriad experiments and a buckshot approach to making and selling. When we met her, she was making over a dozen different cheeses. These days she's totally focused on just three.

My personal favorite, and the one that first won an American Cheese Society blue ribbon and put her on the map, is called Vermont Blue. It's a tall cylinder in the style of a Fourme d'Ambert: tart, sweet, creamy, and a little nutty, like any good meal companion. Her namesake is Gor-Dawn-Zola, her personal take on the Italian classic.

The Green Mountain Farm that the Morin-Bouchers call home uses the time-honored honor system when it comes to retail sales. Pieces in the fridge are wrapped and priced, and the cash can sits on top.

Green Mountain Blue Cheese
2183 Gore Road
Highgate Center, VT 05459
Tel.: 800-447-1205
www.vtcheese.com/vtcheese/greenmtn/vtblue.htm
boucherfarm@hughes.net

CHEESES:

Brother Laurent
Gore-Dawn-Zola
Vermont Blue

CHEESEMAKER:

Dave Smith
Smith's Country Cheese

We walked into the country store–like shop and sidled up to the cheese counter. I came face-to-face with a silver-haired man with sparkling eyes and said, "Haven't we met?" "I think we have," he replied with a smile. "Some years ago you were part of a group that came to Boston to talk about making specialty foods in New England. My wife and I came right back home and started making cheese. Now we have the whole family involved, me and Carol, daughter Jennifer and son John."

Talk about salt of the earth. Smith family cheese is good, honest, plain food. When we visited a few years ago, they were making butter, having some of their cheeses naturally smoked just down the road, and were just generally thrilled with a life of "milk enhancement." Dave had been milking cows for more than thirty years, mostly Holstein, but then later added Normandy breeds, an animal good for beef as well.

Their cheeses are pressed, then brined; no salt is added in the milk or make. They coat the wheels with an edible coating from Holland so as not to stain the cheese the way paraffin will.

Their all-natural cheese spreads were inspired by the fellow they call "the father of cheese spreads," the late Henry Forman from Appleton, Wisconsin, an athletic entrepreneur who had a lab in his basement and a zest for life.

To support the farm and supplement cash flow while continuing to build the business, they keep a couple of hundred extra milkers and let that stock to other farms on contract. Many's the bill paid with the profits from their fertile compost business, made from the three S's—sand, sawdust, and, well, manure.

Smith's Country Cheese, Inc.

20 Otter River Road

Winchendon, MA 01475

Tel.: 800-700-9974

Fax: 978-939-8599

www.smithscountrycheese.com

smithscountrycheese@verizon.net

CHEESES:

Plain Gouda

Smoked Gouda

Gouda with Caraway

Gouda with Cumin

Gouda with Sun-Dried Tomatoes and Basil

Gouda with Garlic

Aged Gouda (one year)

Extra Aged Gouda (two years)

Lite Gouda (Plain and Smoked)

Gouda Spreads

Cheddar (Medium, Sharp, Extra-Sharp)

Rat Cheddar (aged over four years)

Sage Cheddar

Smoked Cheddar

Smith's Farmstead Creamy Havarti

Smoked Havarti

Havarti with Dill

Vegetable Havarti

Bob Stetson
Westfield Farm

"We just saw an ad in the paper . . . always wanted to make something," said Bob Stetson. The former shipping manager from Boston and his wife, Debbie, came along at just the right moment to continue the legacy of some very good cheesemaking.

Hubbardston Blue is a true original, with its blue mold ripening from the outside in. Created by Letty and Bob Kilmoyer a few years before, they have added to this delicate recipe a host of flavored and smoked mostly fresh cheeses.

They got great recipes and solid training, but there have been difficult times as well. On the day of our visit they tried to see if yesterday's culture would work another day, and they lost an entire precious batch. It was a mistake they would never repeat.

Our favorite innovation was the hibachi attached by

a clothes dryer hose to a vintage refrigerator to create a truly memorable cold smoker.

Westfield Farm

28 Worcester Road

Hubbardston, MA 01452

Tel.: 877-777-3900

Fax: 978-928-5745

www.chevre.com

stetson222@verizon.net

CHEESES:

GOAT'S MILK

Plain Capri

Herb Capri

Herb Garlic Capri

Chive Capri

Pepper Capri

Hickory-Smoked Capri

Wasabi Capri

Chocolate Capri

Classic Blue Log

Bluebonnet

White Buck

Goat Cheddar

Hubbardston Blue

Feta Capri

Runny Hubbs

COW'S MILK

Ayrshire Farmer's Cheese

Capri Camembert Cow

Soft/Runny Hubbs

Hubbardston Blue Cow

David Major and Cindy Major
Vermont Shepherd

There is something indomitable about Cindy Major and very New England about her approach to cheese. For Cindy, cheesemaking is a communal, community-wide effort. Her world-class Vermont Shepherd was only part of a long day's work. It's the one cheese she and her former husband, David, made on their farm, but not the only cheese to which they tended.

The Major Farm aging cave was the first I'd seen in this country. The care and thought that went into this simple structure came years into their quest to make really good cheese. Says Cindy, "It took a long time to make good, then great cheese. There's too much alchemy involved."

Cindy grew up in New York, the daughter of a fourth-generation dairy business guy. David grew up across the road from a lot of sheep and farm equipment in Vermont. When they married they wanted to try farming, so they moved to a cabin with his parents down the road.

Raising lamb for wool was really tough, so after a visit to a Vermont state agriculture event, she got a book on practical sheep dairying, almost as a joke. But she gave it a try, and made some really bad cheese. The blue would go veiny. The Gouda got moldy. The feta was atrocious. Cindy couldn't stand the waste, so she

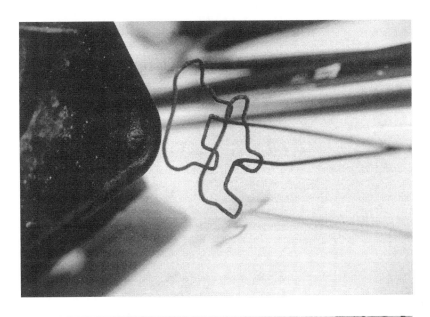

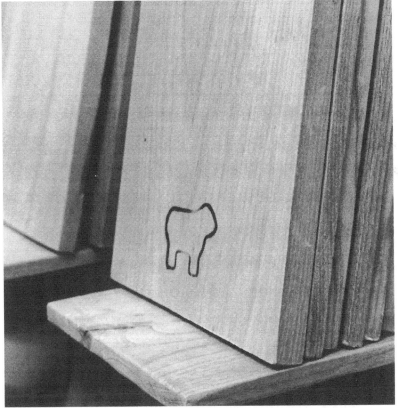

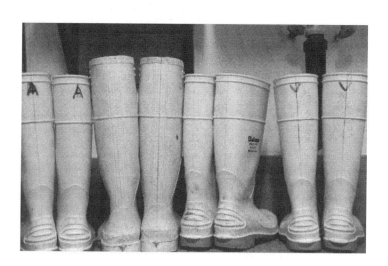

got help from a French farmworker, wrote to Patrick Rance in England, and ended up at a succession of Pyrenees, Basque, and Pau cheesemaking farms. In five years she was making her first good cheese. From that tough start came a commitment to help other cheesemakers, and a good eye—and nose—for ripening many sorts of wheels. Not only did she coax along her own tommes—for a while she even looked after bandage-wrapped cheddars from Shelburne Farms—but she was the first American cheesemaker I know who took in good-quality cheeses that needed a sort of halfway house on the road to greatness. Cindy has left the farm, but her aging cave, Vermont Shepherd, and those early efforts survive.

Vermont Shepherd
875 Patch Road
Putney, VT 05346
Tel.: 802-387-4473
Fax: 802-387-2041
www.vermontshepherd.com
info@vermontshepherd.com

CHEESE:

Vermont Shepherd

CHEESEMAKER:

Elizabeth MacAlister and Mark Gillman
Cato Corner Farm

Occasionally, I get asked to be a judge for awards given to talented
food makers. I'll leave chili cook-offs and strawberry festivals
to stronger stomachs, but I've enjoyed being part of the very
accomplished team behind the Gallo Family Vineyards Gold
Medal Awards for Artisan Foods. We cover a lot of categories,
from condiments to seafood, but the dairy treats are my favorites.

The first year we happened upon a delicious cheese that
seemed somehow familiar. It turned out to be the mother-and-
son-created Hooligan, a "stinky" washed-rind wonder, from
Elizabeth MacAlister and Mark Gillman of Cato Corner Farm in
Colchester, Connecticut.

I'd had it several times before, mostly from their stall at the
Union Square Greenmarket in New York City, but after a few
years of perfecting their craft, this cheese had clearly risen to a
new, complex, and delicious level. What had started out as a noble,
charming family effort had become a big-time, real-deal, first-rate
cheese, tasted blind and heaped with praise by refined palates.

This is truly my kind of food competition. They'd been
challenging themselves to get better, and within a few short years
of long hard work had pleasantly knocked our socks off.

Now they've hit their stride, and every new cheese I taste seems the result of generations of classic cheesemaking. My new favorite is Vivace, and not only because, while delicious, it sounds like the name of well-cut designer jeans.

Cato Corner Farm, LLC

178 Cato Corner Road

Colchester, CT 06415

Tel.: 860-537-3884

Fax: 860-537-9470

www.catocornerfarm.com

catocornerfarm@mindspring.com

info@catocornerfarm.com

CHEESES:

Black Ledge Blue	*Despearado*
Bridgid's Abbey	*Jeremy River Cheddar*
Bloomsday	*Misty Morning*
Aged Bloomsday	*Vivace*
Dutch Farmstead	*Vivace Bambino*
Six-Month-Old Dutch Farmstead	*Molto Vivace*
Hooligan	*Womanchego*
Drunken Hooligan	*Wisewomanchego*
Drunk Monk	

Nancy and Tom Clark
Old Chatham Sheepherding Company

Cheesemakers, and people who love cheesemakers, tend to adore the folks at Old Chatham. There really is nothing like their creamy, rich, mostly sheep's milk soft-ripened cheeses; their sheep and cow's milk Hudson Valley Camembert; those molten Mutton Buttons; their fresh, tangy ricotta; that luscious sheep's milk yogurt.

They've had their fair share of ups and downs. A restaurant didn't work out, but people rallied round and the Old Chatham herd, started with about 150 sheep, now numbers over a thousand. Their familiar (and distinctive) green and black label, on the clean white wrapping, is easy to find in better shops. They also make a classical sheep blue, like a French Roquefort, called Ewe's Blue.

Old Chatham Sheepherding Company
155 Shaker Museum Road
Old Chatham, NY 12136
Tel.: 888-743-3760
Fax: 518-794-7641
www.blacksheepcheese.com
cheese@blacksheepcheese.com

CHEESES:

Hudson Valley Camembert
Nancy's Hudson Valley Camembert
Ewe's Blue Wheel
Mutton Buttons
Ricotta

Douglass Newbold
Greystone Nubians

Douglass Newbold has been making exquisite fresh goat cheese for thirty years. Gently dried in cheesecloth made by local Amish women, lovingly placed in strawberry boxes, and collected to deliver to just a few places, it's obviously a labor of love, with which she's clearly surrounded.

Twice-a-day milking for her eight or nine Nubian girls is carefully watched by a family of animals who live on this picture-perfect, totally natural Pennsylvania farm. The day we were there we saw one of her goats affectionately nibbling the leg of the cat walking along a wooden fence. The steel gray–suede Italian greyhounds were nestled in the barn with the cows. One feisty little terrier stood general guard while another rode, alert on all

fours, on the back of a sleepy donkey. We observed this happening pretty much all at once on what seemed like a regular day.

If you ever come across her Greystone Chevratel cheese, at a nearby restaurant or occasionally at the Reading Terminal Market in Philadelphia, do not fail to taste it. Clouds of sweet goat's milk come to mind.

Greystone Nubians
764 Hillview Road
Malvern, PA 19355
Tel.: 610-296-0463

CHEESE:

Fresh goat cheese

CHEESEMAKER:

Mateo Kehler
Jasper Hill Farm

Mateo Kehler is a first-class cheesemaker. His creamy award-winning Constant Bliss is aptly named (although called that for a Revolutionary War scout by that name who died guarding the supply lines). Their Bayley Hazen Blue, named for that same long-abandoned military road nearby, built by George Washington, seems to—like the road—bring people to the region to discover its splendors.

Mateo, his brother, Andy, and their wives, Victoria and Angela, are rising stars of American cheesemaking with much to offer today and in the years to come.

They have taken up the mantle of Cindy Major's earlier efforts. Even while they slowly build their dreams of a ripening center, they work deftly to bring their own and other cheesemakers' wonderful wheels up to a level only achievable through practice, talent, finesse, and thoughtful collaboration.

Jasper Hill Farm
PO Box 272
Greensboro, VT 05841
www.jasperhillfarm.com
info@jasperhillfarm.com

CHEESES:

Constant Bliss
Bayley Hazen Blue
Aspenhurst

CHEESEMAKER:

Allison Hooper and Bob Reese
Vermont Butter & Cheese

There is something genuine and strong about Allison Hooper. Her dedication to the sometimes fragile dairy industry of Vermont has made her a quiet leader and a constant inspiration.

The fresh chèvre she once produced for a state dinner being thrown by Bob Reese, the man who is now her partner, quickly became a staple for regional restaurants. Their highly regarded cultured butter is used in some of America's top restaurants—including famed chef Thomas Keller's French Laundry in the Napa Valley and Per Se in Manhattan—and her other fresh cheeses, sweet fromage blanc, tangy quark, and rich mascarpone, are not-so-secret ingredients for good cooks wherever these cheeses are found.

Hooper learned cheese and butter making in Brittany. Her practical approach and hopeful spirit have allowed her to succeed and grow in a difficult seasonal business by balancing nature with the marketplace.

We visited just about the time her unique and delicious aged raw milk goat fontina was just getting ready to be sold. You may see it around from time to time, but it's her buttery fresh goat and cow's milk cheeses that remind you how evanescent really good food can be, and how worthwhile. Recently, Allison and Bob have included a collection of handmade cheeses called the Artisan Line. Imagine my delight when I found a platter of Bonne Bouche, Bijou, and Coupole waiting for me in my hotel room, compliments of the chef, very late at night after a miserable Amtrak ride from New York to Washington, D.C.

Vermont Butter & Cheese Company
Websterville, VT 05678
Tel.: 800-884-6287
Fax: 802-479-3674
www.butterandcheese.net
info@vtbutterandcheeseco.com

CHEESES:

GOAT'S MILK	COW'S MILK
Vermont Chèvre	*Crème Fraîche*
Creamy Goat Cheese	*Cultured Butter*
Goat Feta	*Fromage Blanc*
Fresh Crottin	*Mascarpone*
Artisan Line: Bijou, Bonne Bouche, and Coupole	*Quark*

CHEESEMAKER:

Crowley Cheese

It seems to me that they might want to call Wisconsin Colby, Colby Crowley, because the folks at Crowley and many historians tell me that Crowley came first. A sort of washed-curd cousin of cheddar, this clean, simple, humble cheese has been consistently made longer than any other in America.

The rustic plant we visited was built in 1882, and for its time was quite a modern cheesemaking operation. Mr. Crowley's daughter had a beauty parlor on the second floor and the last local namesake was postmaster of Healdville, "over 'cross the way."

The spot is romantic and homey, and a popular stop during foliage season.

Crowley Cheese

14 Crowley Lane

Healdville, VT 05758

Tel.: 800-683-2606

Fax: 802-259-2347

www.crowleycheese.com

sales@crowleycheese.com

CHEESES:

Crowley Colby (Mild, Medium, Sharp, and Extra Sharp)

Sage

Hot Pepper

Smoked

Garlic Chive

Muffaletta

CHEESEMAKER:

Laini Fondiller
Lazy Lady Farm

Our first visit with Laini Fondiller found her up to her ears in cheesemaking. Pots and kettles, curds in molds, small forms being gently flipped—Laini seemed in constant, electric motion, more like a performance artist, with her wild red hair just barely contained, than a lyric country goatherd.

Suddenly the phone gave a loud jangle and Laini found yet another hand to reach for the receiver. "Far out," she hollered to nobody in particular, "they found my cow!" Her new charge had jumped a fence in nervous disorientation soon after she'd arrived.

Life at Lazy Lady Farm is always at least a little experimental, and this was no exception. Proud crafter of more than a dozen distinctly different goat cheeses, Laini was thinking about trying some cow's milk work. Her collection is stunning and a lesson in variety, subtlety, and style of the genre. My favorites are her raw milk cow and goat that are smooth and clean, but all are superior cheeses.

With a recently upgraded facility (now the size of, say, a California king bed instead of a double), she also makes Les Pyramids, Valencay, Capriola, La Roche, and La Petite Tomme.

As for our bovine heroine, "it didn't work out," said Laini some years later. "We ate her, but I kept learning about cows and cheesemaking." And the rest is delicious history.

Lazy Lady Farm
973 Snyderbrook Road
Westfield, VT 05874
Tel.: 802-744-6365
www.vtcheese.com/members/lazylady/lazylady.htm
laini@sover.net

CHEESES:

GOAT'S MILK
Les Pyramids
Valencay
Capriola
La Roche
La Petite Tomme
Mon Jardin
Tomme Delay

COW'S MILK
Holy Cow!
Meadowsweet

Tarte de Force
Buck Hill Sunshine (raw milk)
Buck Hill Sunrise (raw milk)
Fil-a-Buster

MIXED MILK
Demi Tasse
Herbal Essence
Trillium

Cabot Creamery

The historic Cabot Creamery is an example of a cooperative that makes a goodly amount of cheese that still deserves a place on the counter or the plate of any American collection. Their bandage-wrapped aged cheddar is mellow and deep, and some of their special reserve and occasional commemorative cheeses can be world-class.

I've been to Cabot a couple of times. I'll admit to being disquieted by the huge stainless steel holding tanks, and curds that will become forty-pound blocks of cheese in sturdy plastic bags stacked and stored in walk-in refrigerators, but the place has quite a history.

This cooperative started in 1919 when a group of less than a hundred local dairy farmers bought the building and got things going. It was prescient. By 1930 the state had more cows (420,000) than people (just under 360,000), so the cooperative was well prepared.

Things have settled down a lot since then. From a peak of about nine thousand farms, the state now has around two thousand. And now Cabot, along with sizable quantities of mild, buttery standard cheddar, some good five-year-old Old School Cheddar, and a good extra sharp Private Stock Cheddar, has that really wonderful Clothbound Cheddar, these days aged in the cave at Jasper Hill Farms. They sell out, then carefully make more. It's a good tradition.

Cabot Creamery

1 Home Farm Way

Montpelier, VT 05602

Tel.: 888-792-2268

www.cabotcheese.com

info@cabotcheese.com

CHEESES:

Clothbound Cheddar

Old School Cheddar

Vintage Choice Cheddar

Private Stock Cheddar

Classic Vermont Sharp

Smoked Cheddar

Hunter's Cheddar

Cheddar (Mild, Sharp, Extra Sharp, Seriously Sharp)

Reduced-Fat Cheddars

Flavored Cheddars (Chili-Lime Hand-Rubbed, Horseradish, Sun-Dried Tomato Basil, Chipotle, Habanero, Garlic and Herb, Five-Peppercorn)

Monterey Jack

Colby Jack

Pepper Jack

Muenster

Swiss

American

Mozzarella

Parmesan

CHEESEMAKER:

Marjorie Susman and Marian Pollack
Orb Weaver Farm

Marjorie Susman and Marian Pollack have been quietly making exceptional cheese for more than two decades. Finally settling on a formula that works for land and life, their little farm is, like their cheese, named for a truly industrious little spider, the Orb Weaver.

They grow flowers and exquisite vegetables in the greenhouse starting in March, moving out into the garden in the summer, and then make cheese when it's cold outside. The produce, all organic, gets sold to local restaurants and co-ops. The cows, seven for milking and maybe seven more to keep the barn warm, calf in November and are milked twice a day until June. These well-loved bovines summer in the tall grasses, then get with calf again.

For a while they aged some wheels with friends Cindy and David Major, but now they, too, have a little cave. It's a treasure trove.

Their cheese, a raw milk Colby, is that humble giant of their region they now make in separate batches—some in the traditional style of a plain table wheel and others bandage-wrapped and cave-aged for dimension, variety, and depth.

Orb Weaver Farm
3406 Lime Kiln Road
New Haven, VT 05472
Tel.: 802-877-3755
www.orbweaverfarm.com
orbweavr@together.net

CHEESES:

Cave-aged Vermont Farmhouse

Waxed Vermont Farmhouse

CHEESEMAKER:

Shelburne Farms

This spectacular property on the shores of Lake Champlain was
once a Seward-Webb, Vanderbilt-Webb, family getaway. Now it's
a historic landmark and home to some fine cheddar making, some
good educational programs, a lot of visitors (the rooms at the Inn
at Shelburne Farms are pretty swell, if un-air-conditioned), and
some fairly new aging caves.

The most recent head cheesemaker whom I've met, Jaime
Yturriondobeitia, was once a cook at one of my favorite
Burlington, Vermont, bistros, Smokejacks, and the cheese has now
become better than ever.

It's often difficult, when an organization has high ideals and a
broad, complex mission, to accomplish really fine cheesemaking.
Around since only 1980, this is the sort of effort worth supporting,
one that proves that general accessibility can also make room for
talent, quality, subtlety, and depth. Get the clothbound aged cheddar.

Shelburne Farms
1611 Harbor Road
Shelburne, VT 05482
Tel.: 802-985-8686
www.shelburnefarms.org

CHEESES:

Six- to Nine-Month-Old Cheddar	*Three-Year-Old Cheddar*
One-Year-Old Cheddar	*Smoked Cheddar*
Two-Year-Old Cheddar	*Clothbound Cheddar*

CHEESEMAKER:

Scott Fletcher
Grafton Village Cheese

It's a great pleasure to visit the place where they make Grafton Cheddar. The building is welcoming and charming—cows graze out back and a covered bridge creaks nearby—and the cheese is splendid. I've known about this Vermont cheddar for years, but for a long time the only kind I could find was about a year old. If I was lucky, sometimes two.

Through the years of fat phobia that overlaid the 1980s, it was difficult for most cheesemakers to afford the cost of holding, or aging, their cheeses very long. Like some wines made to be enjoyed

soon, cheeses were accessible, simple, and pleasant, if somewhat underdeveloped.

When we stopped by Grafton on a steamy summer's day, the "skeeters" were thick, and the cheese was going on four years old. These days some Five Year Star Select (five years old) makes it across the country to better shops, and there may be even older blocks and wheels on the way soon.

Vermont cheddar often starts buttery and creamy. Pleasing even when young, aging deepens and brings out the flavors you never knew were there.

Grafton Village Cheese Company
PO Box 87
Grafton, VT 05146
Tel.: 800-472-3866
Fax: 802-843-2210
www.graftonvillagecheese.com
info@graftonvillagecheese.com

CHEESES:

Four Star Cheddar (aged four years)
Natural Cheddar (aged one, two, or three years)
Sage Cheddar
Garlic Cheddar
Maple-Smoked Cheddar

Chef Laurent Tourondel

CHEDDAR AND CHIVE BISCUITS

MAKES 8 BISCUITS

These tasty biscuits are served at BLT Fish in Manhattan. The BLT stands for Bistro Laurent Tourondel, and is a nod to things American, as are many of the elements in his big-city restaurants with French structural underpinnings. These biscuits, like his restaurants, are delicious and easy to enjoy.

1½ CUPS ALL-PURPOSE FLOUR, PLUS EXTRA FOR SHAPING

2 TEASPOONS BAKING POWDER

1 TEASPOON SALT

¼ TEASPOON CAYENNE PEPPER

3 TABLESPOONS SOLID VEGETABLE SHORTENING, AT ROOM TEMPERATURE

3 TABLESPOONS UNSALTED BUTTER, AT ROOM TEMPERATURE

1 TABLESPOON CHOPPED FRESH CHIVES

1 CUP GRATED SHARP VERMONT CHEDDAR

1¼ CUPS HEAVY CREAM

COLD UNSALTED BUTTER, SEA SALT, AND MAPLE SYRUP, FOR SERVING

Preheat the oven to 375°F.

Combine the flour, baking powder, salt, and cayenne in a medium bowl. Add the shortening and butter, and with a pastry blender or fork, blend just until the mixture resembles small peas. For tender biscuits, do not overmix. Stir in the chives and cheese. Add the cream and stir in until just blended; be careful not to overmix the dough.

On a lightly floured surface, roll out the dough to a 1-inch thickness. Cut the dough into 2-inch rounds. Place the biscuits on an ungreased baking sheet at least 1½ inches apart. Bake for 15 to 17 minutes or until golden brown.

Serve hot with cold butter sprinkled with sea salt and drizzled with good-quality maple syrup.

Three Mountain Inn (Jamaica, Vt.)

CHEDDAR AND CHIVE STRATA

SERVES 4

On one of our first Vermont wanders, we stayed at this lovely inn run by a young couple determined to enjoy the bed-and-breakfast sort of country life. They suggested we try their version of this old-fashioned heart- (and artery-) stopping and completely satisfying dish. We loved it and so will you.

BUTTER, SOFTENED

½ LOAF FRENCH BREAD, CUBED WITH THE CRUST ON

2 CUPS SHREDDED VERMONT CHEDDAR

2 TABLESPOONS CHOPPED FRESH CHIVES

15 LARGE EGGS

1 TABLESPOON DIJON MUSTARD

5 CUPS HALF-AND-HALF

SALT AND FRESHLY GROUND BLACK PEPPER

Butter a 13 by 9-inch baking pan. Line the pan with the bread. Cover the bread with the cheddar and chives. Whisk together the eggs, mustard, half-and-half, salt, and pepper. Pour over the bread. Cover and refrigerate ideally overnight or for at least 1 hour.

Preheat the oven to 350°F. Bake the strata until golden brown and puffed, about 1 hour. Let sit for 10 minutes to set before serving.

Fanny Mason, Boggy Meadow Farm (Walpole, N.H.)

CREAMY POTATO SOUP

MAKES 8 1-CUP SERVINGS

Potato soup can be warming and transcendent, or bland and chalky. And cheese in soup has always been a little iffy for me; it can have an unpleasant slimy texture. This soup, however, is a happy treat. The sweet and fruity flavors of this New Hampshire cheese bring it all together.

- 2 TABLESPOONS OLIVE OIL
- 2 CUPS THINLY SLICED ONIONS, SCALLIONS, OR LEEKS
- 3 TO 4 TABLESPOONS ALL-PURPOSE FLOUR
- 2 CUPS MILK
- 1 POUND YUKON GOLD POTATOES, PEELED AND SLICED
- 4 CUPS CHICKEN STOCK
- SALT AND FRESHLY GROUND BLACK PEPPER
- 8 OUNCES GRATED BOGGY MEADOW FARM FARMSTEAD BABY SWISS
- FRESH HERBS, FOR GARNISH

Heat the olive oil in a pot. Sweat the onions for 5 to 10 minutes over low heat until translucent. Stir in the flour and milk and cook for 5 minutes more. Add the potatoes and stock and bring to a boil. Reduce to a simmer. Cook for 20 to 30 minutes, until the vegetables are tender.

Remove from the heat and puree in a blender, working in batches if necessary. Season with salt and pepper to taste.

Return the soup to the pot and add the cheese. Heat, stirring, until the cheese is melted. Serve immediately, garnished with your favorite herbs.

Grafton Village Cheese

CHEDDAR CHEESE PUFFS

MAKES 8 TO 10 PUFFS

This is one of those 1950s *Woman's Day* recipes that turns out to be delicious every time. It really is all about the cheese. Go for a good Vermont cheese, like Grafton three, four, or even five years old.

¼ CUP ALL-PURPOSE FLOUR

1 CUP WATER

¼ CUP GRATED GRAFTON CHEDDAR

½ TEASPOON SALT

¼ TEASPOON FRESHLY GROUND BLACK PEPPER

2 TABLESPOONS BUTTER, PLUS EXTRA FOR THE PAN

2 LARGE EGGS

Wet the flour with enough of the water to form a smooth paste. Stir in the cheese, salt, and pepper.

Place the rest of the water and the butter in a pot. Bring to a boil, and when boiling, add the flour mixture. Cook for 3 minutes, stirring constantly. Remove the mixture from the heat, and set aside until cool.

Meanwhile, preheat the oven to 350°F. Add the eggs to the mixture, one at a time. Beat the batter by hand for at least 10 minutes. Butter a baking sheet lightly, and drop the batter onto it, using a heaping teaspoonful for each puff. Leave considerable space between them, as they increase threefold in size.

Bake for 20 minutes. Serve hot.

Cabot Creamery

CHUNKY CHEESE AND CHICKEN SALAD

SERVES 4

This recipe is deceptively simple but really quite delicious. It works well because the cheddar is creamy and sweet, and the tangy Worcestershire adds just the right note. It's one of the few recipes I've included that has cheese with something added, in this case, a nice collection of peppercorns. You can use precooked or leftover chicken breast to save time.

I BONELESS, SKINLESS CHICKEN BREAST, SPLIT

WORCESTERSHIRE SAUCE

3 TO 4 OUNCES CABOT FIVE-PEPPERCORN CHEDDAR CHEESE OR OTHER CABOT CHEDDAR, CUBED

3 TO 4 OUNCES CABOT SHARP CHEDDAR CHEESE, CUBED

6 CUPS TORN ROMAINE LETTUCE

½ CUP CAESAR SALAD DRESSING, HOMEMADE OR STORE-BOUGHT

½ CUP CROUTONS

½ CUP GRATED CABOT PARMESAN CHEESE

The Northeast and New England

Grill or simmer the chicken for 10 to 15 minutes, until cooked through. Sprinkle lightly with Worcestershire sauce. Cut into strips and set aside.

In a large bowl, toss together the cheeses, lettuce, dressing, and croutons.

Arrange on four salad plates.

Top with the chicken strips and sprinkle with the Parmesan cheese.

Marian Burros, Cooking for Comfort

MACARONI AND CHEESE

SERVES 3 OR 4 AS A MAIN DISH OR 6 AS A SIDE DISH

This is a recipe I've given away and taken back any number of times. I'm personally devoted to mac and cheese, and the genesis of this came from a restaurant where I was a partner in the mid-1990s. But it really came into its own when it was redeveloped for the SoHo Grand Hotel in Manhattan, then morphed into a more home-kitchen-friendly version by Marian Burros for her wonderful, friendly book *Cooking for Comfort*.

I CUP DICED ONION

2 TABLESPOONS UNSALTED BUTTER

2 TABLESPOONS UNBLEACHED ALL-PURPOSE FLOUR

2 CUPS LOW-FAT MILK

I TABLESPOON DIJON MUSTARD

12 OUNCES GRATED EXTRA SHARP AGED WHITE CHEDDAR

SALT AND FRESHLY GROUND WHITE PEPPER

1/2 TEASPOON GROUND NUTMEG

1/4 TEASPOON HOT PEPPER SAUCE (OR TO TASTE)

8 OUNCES CAVATAPPI OR OTHER CORKSCREW PASTA

2 TABLESPOONS GRATED PARMIGIANO-REGGIANO

Preheat the oven to 400°F. Place a rack in the bottom third of the oven.

In a large saucepan, cook the onion in the butter over low heat for 5 to 7 minutes, until the onion is soft but not browned. Stir in the flour. Remove from the heat and whisk in the milk until thoroughly blended. Return to medium heat and cook, stirring, until the mixture begins to thicken. Remove from the heat and stir in the mustard and 10 ounces (2½ cups) of the cheddar, salt, pepper, the nutmeg, and hot pepper sauce.

Meanwhile, cook the pasta according to the package directions until just al dente. Drain but do not rinse. Stir immediately into the cheese sauce until well blended. Adjust the seasoning.

Spoon the mixture into a 13 by 9-inch baking dish. Top with the remaining 2 ounces cheddar and the Parmigiano-Reggiano. Bake for about 30 minutes, until the mixture is hot, bubbling throughout, and golden.

NOTES: The casserole can be refrigerated before baking. Let the dish return to room temperature and follow the baking directions.

The quality and sharpness of the cheese are all-important to the success of this dish. Use a white cheddar that has been aged at least two years. Grafton Village cheese is always my choice.

Old Chatham Sheepherding Company

HUDSON VALLEY CAMEMBERT CRISP

SERVES 4

This cheese proves that the whole is greater than the sum of its parts. The sheep's milk gives the cheese body and depth; cow's milk makes it creamy. Together, in this soft-ripened cheese wrapped in dough and crisped, they become oozing heaven. Serve the packets on a bed of fairly firm greens—even some slightly bitter ones, like chicory, Treviso, or radicchio—or some crisp endive and peppery cress accompanied by a fruit chutney and toasted crusty bread. Serve with a knife, a fork, and a spoon.

TWO 4-OUNCE HUDSON VALLEY CAMEMBERT
   SQUARES

3 SHEETS PHYLLO DOUGH

2 TABLESPOONS MELTED BUTTER

1 LARGE EGG, MIXED WITH 1 TEASPOON WATER,
   FOR EGG WASH

1 TABLESPOON BUTTER

Cut each Camembert diagonally into two triangles. Set aside.

Lay a sheet of phyllo on your work surface. Butter lightly and lay another sheet over the top. Repeat with the third sheet, brushing the top with butter. Cut lengthwise into four strips.

Place one Camembert triangle at the bottom of a strip. Beginning at the bottom, start rolling the phyllo and the cheese up, folding the phyllo over the cheese, like making spanakopita. Brush the final fold with a little egg wash to seal it. Repeat with the remaining cheese triangles and phyllo strips.

When ready to serve, heat a skillet over medium heat. Melt the butter and brown the cheese packets on all sides until golden. Serve warm.

Chef Marcus Samuelsson

BLACK PEPPER CHEESECAKE

SERVES 10 TO 12

Marcus Samuelsson, the chef of New York's famed Aquavit and other restaurants, is an Ethiopian-born Swede who has been named one of *People* magazine's fifty most beautiful people. He is also an extraordinarily talented chef. His food is refined and subtle, so when he gets spicy, the impact is memorable. Here's a recipe I would only trust, or even try, from someone as good as this chef is in the kitchen.

1 ½ TEASPOONS BLACK PEPPERCORNS

12 OUNCES CHAMPLAIN VALLEY CREAMERY ORGANIC CREAM CHEESE, AT ROOM TEMPERATURE

⅓ CUP SUGAR

1 VANILLA BEAN, SPLIT LENGTHWISE IN HALF

¾ CUP CRÈME FRAÎCHE, SOUR CREAM, OR WHOLE-MILK YOGURT

2 TABLESPOONS FRESHLY SQUEEZED LEMON JUICE

2 LARGE EGGS

1 ½ CUPS HEAVY CREAM

Preheat the oven to 250°F. Spray an 8-inch round cake pan with nonstick cooking spray. Line the bottom with a round of parchment paper and spray the parchment paper.

Blanch the peppercorns in a small saucepan of boiling water for 1 minute; drain. Repeat two more times. Pat the peppercorns dry with paper towels. Spread the peppercorns in a small baking pan and dry them in the oven for 15 to 20 minutes, until thoroughly dry. Remove from the oven and let cool. Turn the oven up to 350°F.

Grind the peppercorns medium-fine in a spice grinder or a clean coffee grinder, or use a mortar and pestle; set aside.

Beat the cream cheese and sugar with an electric mixer on medium-high speed for about 3 minutes, until very smooth and light. Scrape the seeds from the vanilla bean and add to the cream cheese mixture. Beat in the crème fraîche and scrape down the sides of the bowl. Add the lemon juice. Add the eggs one at a time, beating well after each addition and scraping down the sides of the bowl as necessary. Beat in the cream and ground peppercorns.

Scrape the batter into the prepared pan. Set the pan inside a large shallow baking pan and pour about 1 inch of hot water into the larger pan. Bake for 1 hour, or until the sides of the cake are set but the center is still a little loose. Transfer the cake pan to a wire rack to cool completely.

When the cheesecake is cool, cover with plastic wrap and refrigerate overnight.

To unmold the cheesecake, run a thin knife or spatula around the sides of the pan. Set the pan on a hot burner for about 20 seconds, shaking the pan gently from side to side to release the cake. Invert the cake onto a cake plate, peel off the parchment, and serve.

Vermont Butter & Cheese Company

ROASTED BOSC PEARS WITH SPIKED VERMONT MASCARPONE

SERVES 4

Stuffed and baked fruit is a particularly satisfying winter tradition in many parts of America. This recipe feels modern and classic at the same time, and shows off the buttery nature of Vermont's cheeses.

- 4 BOSC PEARS
- 2 TABLESPOONS UNSALTED BUTTER, SOFTENED
- 2 TABLESPOONS DARK BROWN SUGAR
- ½ CUP MARSALA WINE
- ½ CUP DRY WHITE WINE
- 2 CINNAMON STICKS
- ¼ CUP MAPLE SYRUP
- ½ TEASPOON GRATED LEMON ZEST
- I CUP VERMONT BUTTER & CHEESE COMPANY MASCARPONE
- CONFECTIONERS' SUGAR, FOR GARNISH

Preheat the oven to 325°F.

Trim the bottoms from the pears and with a corer, remove the core and seeds. Rub the butter over the pears. Stand the pears upright in a shallow baking dish. Sprinkle the brown sugar over the pears and drizzle with both wines. Add the cinnamon sticks to the baking dish. Cover with aluminum foil and bake for 30 to 45 minutes, until the pears are very soft. Remove the pears from the oven and let cool.

Gently stir the maple syrup and lemon zest into the mascarpone. To serve, mound the mascarpone mixture in the center of four dessert plates. Place a roasted pear on top of each mound and drizzle with the pan juices. Lightly dust each pear with confectioners' sugar and serve.

BERKSHIRE BLUE CHEESE BREAD PUDDING

There was a time when a bread pudding made with dirt would have been a hit on a restaurant menu. Many of them are still stuck in my craw, but this is one of the few in the savory column that's easy to love. You might want to serve this alongside a nice crisp mixed green salad, enjoy the meal, and then go for a 10-kilometer run, at the very least.

2 TABLESPOONS MELTED BUTTER

½ LOAF FRENCH BREAD, CUT INTO ½-INCH CUBES, WITH CRUST

1 TABLESPOON PORCINI POWDER (SEE NOTE)

1 TO 2 TABLESPOONS PORCINI OIL (SEE NOTE), TO TASTE

SALT AND FRESHLY GROUND BLACK PEPPER

8 LARGE EGGS

4 LARGE EGG YOLKS

4 CUPS MILK

¼ CUP OLIVE OIL

½ CUP DICED LEEKS (USE REMAINING GREEN AND WHITE PARTS AFTER TOP 2 INCHES ARE DISCARDED)

2 CLOVES ELEPHANT GARLIC, MINCED

1 POUND MIXED FRESH WILD MUSHROOMS, CLEANED AND ROUGHLY CHOPPED

1 POUND BERKSHIRE BLUE, CRUMBLED

Preheat the oven to 350°F. Brush a 13 by 9-inch glass baking dish with the melted butter.

Spread the bread cubes in the baking dish in an even layer. Sprinkle the porcini powder, porcini oil, and salt and pepper over the bread cubes. Set aside.

Combine the eggs and egg yolks in a medium heatproof bowl. Scald the milk in a 2-quart saucepan. Carefully pour the hot milk into the eggs, stirring constantly.

Heat the olive oil in a large sauté pan until the oil shimmers. Sauté the leeks, garlic, and mushrooms for 6 to 8 minutes, until tender. Add to the custard.

Pour the custard-mushroom mixture over the bread. Sprinkle evenly with the cheese. Cover with foil. Bake for 40 minutes, or until set. Let cool for 20 minutes before serving.

NOTE: Porcini powder and porcini oil are available at www.zingermans.com and at most specialty food stores.

Many of the cheeses in the Northeast have strong European influences, but new ones, sometimes in less traditional forms, are popping up all the time.

We came upon **Does' Leap** fresh goat cheese one summer afternoon in Burlington, Vermont. George Van Vlaanderen and Kristan Doolan had been making it for barely three weeks. It's a good example of how small producers of good, fresh goat cheese are popping up all over the country.

Then there's **Wölffer Estate Vineyard** on Long Island, New York. They make some nice wines and, in small quantities mostly for visitors, family, and locals, a delicious Gruyère that we tasted on a visit to the East End a few years ago. I don't even know if they actually sell it to the public, but look for more wineries to get involved in cheese production around the country.

Bufala di Vermont, Vermont Water Buffalo, Inc., in Vermont makes creamy and flavorful yogurts.

Berkshire Blue cheese was developed over a dozen-year process beginning in England and ending with it now being made in Great Barrington, Massachusetts. Other than the truck that delivers the milk and the heating and refrigeration equipment, there are no mechanical devices involved in the cheesemaking. It is done entirely by hand. The loving care and classical methods yield wonderful blue-veined results.

Great Hill Blue is made from unhomogenized raw cow's milk cheese in Marion, Massachusetts. The wheels are internally ripened with a slightly more dense and yellow curd than some others.

There seems to be an explosion of cheesemaking in Maine. Much of it is staying close to home; a lot of it is very good. **York Hill Farm** has been making goat cheeses for nearly twenty-five years. The fresh varieties, with or without herbs, are appealing, as is the nearly year-aged Capriano.

For sheep's (as well as goat's and cow's) milk cheeses, there's **Appleton Creamery** in Appleton, Maine. My favorite is BreBrie—a soft-ripening, bloomy-rind sheep's milk award winner.

Does' Leap
1703 Route 108 South
East Fairfield, VT 05448
Tel.: 802-827-3046
Fax: 501-325-8818
www.doesleap.com
doesleap@verizon.com

Wölffer Estate Vineyard
139 Sagg Road
PO Box 9002
Sagaponack, NY 11962
Tel.: 631-537-5106
www.wolffer.com

Bufala di Vermont
2749-01 Church Hill Road
South Woodstock, VT 05071
Tel.: 802-457-4540
Fax: 802-457-4541
www.bufaladivermont.com
info@bufaladivermont.com

Berkshire Blue
PO Box 2021
Lenox, MA 01240
Tel.: 413-528-9529
www.berkshireblue.com

Great Hill Blue
160 Delano Road
Marion, MA 02738
Tel.: 888-748-2208
www.greathillblue.com

Appleton Creamery
780 Gurney Town Road
Appleton, ME 04862
www.appletoncreamery.com

York Hill Farm
257 York Hill Road
New Sharon, ME 04955
Tel.: 207-778-9741
207-778-2646

American Cheeses

The South

I'M NOT REALLY SURE EXACTLY WHERE the South begins. It seems to start somewhere just below Philadelphia and wander down all the way to some part of Texas.

America's first cows were Jerseys, brought to the Jamestown colony in Virginia, but they're rarely identified with the southern states. Today, many of the leading and sought-after cheesemakers in the region favor goats, although cow's milk does once again play a strong local role.

At the American Cheese Society conference in 2005, with July sneaking up to August in downtown Louisville, Kentucky, a passionate group gathered to talk about regional cheese guilds. One woman spoke from her position as a key organizer of the southern contingent, so I had a chance to ask her what style, what sensibilities and approach, did her regional colleagues seem to share. In what ways were they somehow regionally unifiable and identifiable?

She tilted her head gently and, without a morsel of malicious intent, looked me straight in the eye and said, "Absolutely no way at all. We're each completely different."

She seems to be right. When it comes to cheesemaking, it really ought to be called the Independent South.

CHEESEMAKER:

Judy Schad
Capriole Farmstead Goat Cheese

Sometimes becoming a cheesemaking family feels a lot like coming home. Occasionally it really is. When Judy Schad and her husband, Larry, were looking for a spread to settle on, they crossed the Ohio River at New Albany, Indiana, and started to wander.

Suddenly Larry felt something like déjà vu: the farm that seemed so right for them had once upon a time belonged to his great-great-grandfather. Part of a former Lewis and Clark land grant, his family

had owned and worked it from about 1850 to sometime in the 1930s or '40s, when they lost the farm during the Depression. Schad Springs was nearby, but nobody had made the connection. The land wasn't exactly Eden— not particularly fertile, hilly, and fairly rocky. Goats, thought Judy, goats.

Judy Schad started making cheese in her

kitchen in the early 1980s. She took a class from Ricki Carroll (see page 53) at a goat conference in Dekalb, Illinois, and her interest turned to passion.

But it was working for pioneering cheesemakers Letty and Bob Kilmoyer, original owners of Westfield Farm in Massachusetts (where they created the American original Hubbardston Blue in 1987), that the deeper skill sets took hold. "I still make a vat of cheese the way I learned then," says Schad. "I had the best training."

By 1990 Judy and Larry had built a plant right on their farm, mainly focusing on fresh goat cheese, sometimes with herbs and spices mixed in—"anything to sell cheese and pay the bills," Judy recalls. "Pesto and pine nuts . . . it was nasty."

In the mid-1990s she had a sort of creative explosion with five new cheeses in one year. "I was insane," says Judy. When her friend and mentor Chantal Plasse suggested she do something different, what the French call a *boule,* her Wabash Cannonball was born.

Judy is hard-working, completely dedicated, and determined. She's generous with her time and talents, and though Ed Behr (the author of *The Art of Eating* quarterly) may have been quoting a cliché when he wrote "The goat is the cow of the poor," her spirit is rich and her life full, with family and friends and that beautiful rediscovered farm.

Capriole Farmstead Goat Cheese

PO Box 117

10329 Newcut Road

Greenville, IN 47124

Tel.: 812-923-9408

Fax: 812-923-8901

www.capriolegoatcheese.com

caprioleinc@aol.com

CHEESES:

SURFACE RIPENED

Wabash Cannonball

Piper's Pyramide

Crocodile Tear

Sofia

FRESH GOAT

Chantal Aperitifs

Blue River Buttons

Chèvre

AGED/RAW MILK

Old Kentucky Tomme

Mont St. Francis

Julianna

SPECIALTY

O'Banon

Fromage à Trois

CHEESEMAKER:

John Folse
Bittersweet Plantation Dairy

Since Hurricane Katrina, many of us have worried about preserving the traditions of southern Louisiana and how they will be kept alive without the thriving excesses of New Orleans. We needn't. Not only will that great city rise again, in its own way and time, but we have John Folse, near Baton Rouge, keeping an eye on things.

Chef Folse has been a tireless crusader for all things culinary, Louisianan, American, and delicious for years. His wildly acclaimed Lafayette Landing Restaurant was a huge hit, and in 2002 he opened the Bittersweet Plantation Dairy.

I particularly like their Fleur-de-Teche, a triple crème cow's milk cheese with a line of ash wandering through it, like the waterway of Bayou Teche, for which it's named. It's delicious.

The dairy makes Creole Cream Cheese, a blend of skim milk and half-and-half that was unavailable for years but now is blessedly back.

They've added some goat feta and a delicious couple of little chèvres, named for the tragic lovers Evangeline and Gabriel from Longfellow's poem, that age into worthy goods. I guess the right kind of mold really does thrive down that way.

Bittersweet Plantation Dairy

2517 South Philippe Avenue

Gonzales, LA 70737

Tel.: 225-644-6000

Fax: 225-647-0316

www.jfolse.com/bittersweet_dairy/products.htm

folse@jfolse.com

CHEESES:

GOAT'S MILK

Evangeline

Gabriel

Bulgarian-Style Feta

COW'S MILK

Fleur-de-Lis Fromage Triple Cream

Fleur-de-Teche Fromage Triple Cream with Vegetable Ash

Creole Cream Cheese

Holy Cow—Vache Santé

MIXED MILK

Feliciana Nevat

The South

Mike Koch and Pablo Solanet
FireFly Farms

You can never tell about people. Sometimes they're fun and enthusiastic, charming and smart, but just can't make good food to save their lives. You worry that they have what Gerald Asher, long-time and legendary wine editor of *Gourmet* magazine, used to call Polaroid syndrome. You know, "Here's a picture of me with my goats" and "Here's one with our first cheese." You worry that all good intentions, and not a little money, will go for naught.

Well, the buff boys at FireFly Farms have proved my worries groundless. While Mike Koch has had (and continues) a full career in finance at Fannie Mae, he comes by dairy work honestly, as grandson of an Iowa dairy farmer who emigrated from the Alpine foothills of Switzerland, from generations of cheesemakers. Pablo Solanet, from glamorous Buenos Aires, is a trained chef (mostly a pastry maven) and cheese technologist who elevates chemistry to craft.

My favorite of this growing collection is their American Cheese Society award-winning Mountain Top Bleu, a flat-topped little pyramid with blue and white mold on the outside and some blue veining throughout the whole cheese. It's creamy and flavorful, blue, and mildly goaty.

FireFly Farms

1363 Brenneman Road

Bittinger, MD 21522

Tel.: 301-245-4630

Fax: 800-343-1761

www.fireflyfarms.com

info@fireflyfarms.us

CHEESES:

Allegheny Chèvre

Mountain Top Bleu

Merry Goat Round

Bûche Noire

Meadow Chèvre

CHEESEMAKER:

Paula Lambert
Mozzarella Company

For the twentieth anniversary of Dallas's Mozzarella Company, a whole lot of family and friends gathered in the gussied-up parking lot next door to Paula Lambert's little cheese factory. As potentially contradictorily amazing as the name (oh, and that party) might seem, Paula is the Queen of Texas and one of the true stars of American cheesemaking.

She has a way with a surprisingly broad range of well-made cheeses—more than thirty in all—in part because for a long while she was the only game in town, and if a walk-in customer or the cousin of a former schoolmate—in fact, *anyone*—needed something that she didn't have, if she could make it, she did.

I loved watching her make a very unique and delicious Oaxaca, a pulled-curd Mexican string cheese—cousin of mozzarella—that she pulled warm, laid on long trays, and sprinkled with freshly squeezed Mexican limes, before winding into the signature twisted balls they become.

She also still makes a few addictive mascarpone tortas, a mild blue mold (outside only) Deep Ellum Blue, a few more very special Hispanic-inspired cheeses, some Italian-style ones, and fresh Texas goat cheese. She's written two really lovely books, *The Cheese Lover's Cookbook and Guide* and *Cheese, Glorious Cheese!*

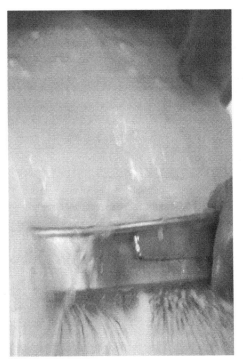

Paula's silvery hair, sparkling eyes, peppery drawl, and enormous heart are only surpassed by her focused will and wonderful talents for making and sharing a world of cheese. I just love her to bits.

Mozzarella Company

2944 Elm Street

Dallas, TX 75226

Tel.: 800-798-2954

www.mozzco.com

contact@mozzco.com

CHEESES:

COW'S MILK

Baby Caciotta

Burrata

Chile Caciotta

Herb Caciotta

Plain Caciotta

Blanca Bianca

Caciocavallo

Cream Cheese

Crème Fraîche

Crescenza

Feta

Fromage Blanc

Mascarpone

Mascarpone Tortas

Montasio

Rosemary Montasio

Montasio Festivo

Queso Blanco

Queso Blanco with Serrano
Chiles and Epazote

Queso Fresco

Ricotta

Sweet Cream Butter

Deep Ellum Blue

Triple Crème Cheese

Mozzarella

Bocconcini

Latte

Mozzarella Rolls

Smoked Mozzarella

Smoked Scamorza

Queso Oaxaca

Mozzarella Curd

GOAT'S MILK

Soft

Pieces

Herb Logs

Goat Caciotta

Goat Feta

Fromage Blanc

Hoja Santa Goat Cheese Bundles

Ricotta

MIXED MILK

Capriella

CHEESEMAKER:

Jeremy Little
Sweet Grass Dairy

I was in Atlanta with a pride of food, travel, and lifestyle writers looking at how that great southern city is part of a national phenomenon of local, regional, national, and international crossroads culture when it comes to modern cooking and the American table.

Working with the California Walnut Board, I'd been with groups in Seattle, the Hudson Valley, western Sonoma County, and Sacramento. They were tasty, enlightening trips.

We ambled into Anne Quatrano and Clifford Harrison's lovely Star Provisions, a food shopper's paradise and a great retail and wholesale solution for the talented duo to ensure that their well-regarded restaurants—Bacchanalia, Quinones, and Float Away Café—stay well stocked with precious ingredients. This retail emporium is a logical, profitable extension of their vision and an appealing public larder.

It's a series of small spaces around a large warehouselike room full of stylish country dry goods. The meats are stellar and the bakery a dream, but it's the dairy room just off and behind the coffee bean counter that gets me every time.

A smiling, fresh-faced clerk waved at us as we walked in. "The Sweet Grass Dairy is here," she called out to us. It was the first arrival of the season's fresh chèvre from down the way in Thomasville, Georgia.

It's just one of the specialties of the award-winning cheese-making Wehner family. They do a double-cream, soft-ripened, cow's milk Green Hill; the popular, seasonal, and very limited Asher Blue; and a few others. But it's the fresh chèvre that connects them to the twenty-first-century American artisan network. It's a model we've seen over and over: local tradition combined with modern, top-quality, artisan foods that leads to the kind of melting pot that makes America proud.

Sweet Grass Dairy

19635 US Highway 19N

Thomasville, GA 31792

Tel.: 229-227-0752

Fax: 229-227-6170

www.sweetgrassdairy.com

info@sweetgrassdairy.com

CHEESES:

COW'S MILK	GOAT'S MILK
Green Hill	*Lumiere*
Asher Blue	*Fresh Chèvre*
Mediterranean Feta	*Georgia Pecan Chèvre*
Thomasville Tomme	*Holly Springs*
Heat	*Holly Springs with Herbs*
Sevenwood	

Loews Miami Beach Hotel

PROVOLETTA, TOMATO, ROASTED GARLIC, OREGANO, AND CROSTINI

SERVES 1

In Buenos Aires and other parts of Argentina, a slab of provolone is slathered with olive oil and tossed on the *parilla,* otherwise known as the grill. Here, a slightly grander and almost main course (or luncheon with a salad) version comes from the Gaucho Room, a South American–style grand grill I helped create at the Loews Miami Beach Hotel. The restaurant buzzed happily along until it was leased to some friendly fellow from Massachusetts by way of New Orleans who says "Bam" a lot and can certainly fill a dining room.

Oregano Oil

> ½ CUP EXTRA VIRGIN OLIVE OIL
>
> ½ CUP CHOPPED FRESH OREGANO
>
> KOSHER SALT

Herb Crostini

> ½ CUP EXTRA VIRGIN OLIVE OIL
>
> ½ CUP MINCED FRESH HERBS OF CHOICE
>
> KOSHER SALT AND FRESHLY GROUND BLACK PEPPER
>
> 1 BAGUETTE SLICE, ¼ INCH THICK
>
> ABOUT ½ CUP GRATED PARMIGIANO-REGGIANO CHEESE

Provoletta

2 1/2 OUNCES PROVOLONE CHEESE,
   CUT IN A TRIANGLE

MELTED BUTTER

CORNMEAL

Garnish

4 SLICES TOMATO CONFIT (SEE NOTE)

5 CLOVES ROASTED GARLIC (SEE NOTE), SQUEEZED

1/2 OUNCE RED RADISH SPROUTS

FRESHLY SQUEEZED LEMON JUICE

For the oregano oil, whisk together the oil and oregano. Season with salt. This may be held up to 48 hours, tightly covered, in the refrigerator.

For the herb crostini, preheat the oven to 400°F. Blend the oil, herbs, and salt and pepper to taste in a small bowl. Toss the bread in the mixture until well coated. Place on a baking sheet and sprinkle with the cheese. Toast in the oven for 3 to 5 minutes, until golden brown and crisp. Keep warm.

For the provoletta, heat a grill to high. Dip the provolone in melted butter and coat lightly with cornmeal. Grill for 1 minute, turning once. Transfer to an ovenproof plate and bake until completely melted, 2 to 3 minutes. Reshape the melted cheese into a triangle in the center of the plate. Arrange the tomato slices and garlic around the cheese. Toss the radish sprouts with a few drops of lemon juice and place on top of the cheese. Drizzle with 2 tablespoons of the oregano oil. Place the crostini on the side of the plate and serve immediately.

NOTE: Tomato Confit: Dip a whole tomato into boiling water for 10 seconds, place in an ice bath to chill, and peel the skin. Cut the tomato into 8 wedges and remove the pulp. Place 1 tablespoon of olive oil in a baking pan, add 4 of the tomato wedges, and sprinkle with salt and pepper. Roast in the oven at 160°F for 1½ hours.

NOTE: Roasted Garlic: Cut off the top of a garlic bulb, drizzle the garlic with olive oil, and season with a pinch of salt and pepper. Wrap the garlic in foil and bake at 350°F until fork tender, about 20 minutes.

Chef Dean Fearing
Mansion on Turtle Creek (Dallas)

CHEDDAR CHEESE AND POBLANO CHILE SOUP WITH CRISP CHEESE CRACKERS

SERVES 4

This recipe was originally created when Dean Fearing was chef at the legendary Mansion on Turtle Creek in Dallas, where he helped put Texas on the culinary map more than two decades ago. Now he's at the helm of his own gem of a dining palace, Fearing's, not far away. This is the sort of recipe that shows how Dean has refined a familiar dish, making it perfect for a well-grounded special occasion. Kind of like staying in a good, solid five-star hotel.

1 TABLESPOON BACON FAT

1 ONION, CHOPPED

3 SHALLOTS, CHOPPED

1 CLOVE GARLIC, CHOPPED

1 JALAPEÑO CHILE, SEEDED AND CHOPPED

1/2 TEASPOON CHILI POWDER

2 TEASPOONS CHOPPED FRESH CILANTRO

1 TEASPOON CHOPPED FRESH EPAZOTE, OR
  1 TEASPOON DRIED

PINCH OF GROUND CUMIN

3/4 CUP BEER

7 CUPS CHICKEN STOCK (PAGE 127)

4 TABLESPOONS (1/2 STICK) UNSALTED BUTTER,
  SOFTENED

1/4 CUP ALL-PURPOSE FLOUR

2 POBLANO CHILES, SEEDED
  AND CUT INTO 1/4-INCH DICE

4 CUPS SHREDDED CHEDDAR CHEESE

SALT

FRESHLY SQUEEZED LIME JUICE

Heat the bacon fat in a large sauté pan over medium heat. When hot, add the onion, shallots, garlic, jalapeño, and chili powder and sauté for 2 minutes, or until the vegetables are soft. Add the cilantro, epazote, cumin, and beer and bring to a boil. Boil for about 5 minutes, until the liquid has reduced by half. Add the chicken stock and bring to a boil, skimming the foam from the top. Knead the butter and flour together, then slowly whisk into the boiling soup, mixing until smooth. Reduce the heat and simmer for about 40 minutes.

Meanwhile, prepare a smoker for cold smoke. Smoke the poblanos for 10 to 12 minutes. Reserve. Remove the soup from the heat and immediately stir in the cheese. Pour into a blender and process until smooth. (Work in batches if necessary.) Add the reserved poblanos and season with salt and lime juice. Pour into warm soup bowls and serve immediately with Crisp Cheese Crackers (page 126) on the side.

CRISP CHEESE CRACKERS

4 CUPS ALL-PURPOSE FLOUR

½ CUP CORNMEAL

1 TABLESPOON KOSHER SALT

1 TEASPOON CAYENNE PEPPER

½ TEASPOON COARSELY GROUND BLACK PEPPER

16 TABLESPOONS (2 STICKS) UNSALTED BUTTER, CUBED AND FROZEN

10 OUNCES WHITE CHEDDAR CHEESE, GRATED (ABOUT 1½ CUPS)

2 CUPS WHOLE MILK

Combine the flour, cornmeal, salt, cayenne pepper, and black pepper in the mixing bowl of a stand mixer with a paddle. Add the cubed frozen butter and mix until the butter resembles pebbles. Add the cheese and the milk until a dough forms.

Roll into logs about 2 inches in diameter and wrap first in parchment paper and then in plastic wrap. Place the dough in the freezer for about 2 hours, or until firm enough to slice.

Preheat the oven to 325°F. Remove the logs from the freezer and allow to thaw slightly. Slice the dough very thin and bake on lightly greased baking sheets until golden brown. Remove from the baking sheets and cool on racks until crisp.

Chicken Stock

    1 CHICKEN CARCASS

    2 TABLESPOONS CORN, PEANUT, OR VEGETABLE OIL

    2 CUPS COARSELY CHOPPED ONIONS

    ¾ CUP COARSELY CHOPPED CARROTS

    ¾ CUP COARSELY CHOPPED CELERY

    3 SPRIGS FRESH THYME

    3 SPRIGS FRESH PARSLEY

    1 SMALL BAY LEAF

    1 TABLESPOON WHITE PEPPERCORNS

    WATER TO COVER (ABOUT 5 CUPS)

Cut the carcass into small pieces, using a cleaver. Heat
1 tablespoon of the oil in a large pot over medium heat. Add
the carcass. Cook, stirring often, until well browned.

Add the remaining 1 tablespoon oil and the onions, carrots, and
celery. Cook, stirring frequently, until the vegetables are golden
brown. Pour off the oil. Add the thyme, parsley, bay leaf, and
peppercorns. Stir to blend and add water to cover.

Bring to a boil, reduce the heat, and simmer for 1½ to 2 hours,
skimming the surface as necessary, until reduced to 4 cups.

Strain through an extra-fine sieve, pushing on the solids to extract
as much liquid as possible. Discard the solids. Skim off any surface
fat. Refrigerate, tightly sealed, for no more than 2 days, or freeze
for up to 3 months.

Chef Robert Del Grande, Cafe Annie (Houston)

CHIPOTLE–BLUE CHEESE DRESSING

MAKES ABOUT 2 ½ CUPS

This dressing is so simple and delicious that I tend to want to make it first, then find something to pour it over. A crisp salad, a really rare rib-eye steak, or a mesquite wood–grilled chicken comes immediately to mind, or it can go over the recipe that follows.

> 2 LARGE SHALLOTS, UNPEELED
>
> 1 CUP MAYONNAISE
>
> ½ CUP BUTTERMILK
>
> 1 CUP CRUMBLED ARTISAN BLUE CHEESE SUCH AS GREAT HILL BLUE FROM MARION, MASS.
>
> 1 CHIPOTLE CANNED IN ADOBO, MINCED
>
> 2 TEASPOONS ADOBO SAUCE (FROM CANNED CHIPOTLES)
>
> ¼ TEASPOON FRESHLY GROUND BLACK PEPPER
>
> ½ TEASPOON SALT

Preheat the oven to 350°F. In a baking dish, roast the shallots until tender and lightly caramelized. Remove from the oven and when cool enough to handle, peel and mince the shallots.

Combine the shallots, mayonnaise, buttermilk, blue cheese, chipotle, adobo sauce, pepper, and salt and mix well. Store in the refrigerator.

Serve as a salad dressing, a dip, or a sauce for meats.

Chef Robert Del Grande, Cafe Annie *(Houston)*

CHILE CON QUESO "BEYOND TEX-MEX"

SERVES 4 TO 6

Here's a high/low combination that can't be beat. It's a recipe for those who just can't quite kick the creamy habit of a Texas staple, enhanced with some of the best artisan cheddar around.

> 1 OR 2 JALAPEÑO CHILES
>
> 4 OUNCES VELVEETA, CUT INTO 1-INCH CUBES
>
> 4 OUNCES ARTISAN CHEDDAR CHEESE, SUCH AS BRAVO FARMS WHITE CHEDDAR (FROM TRAVER, CALIF.), CUT INTO 1-INCH CUBES
>
> ½ CUP HALF-AND-HALF, PLUS EXTRA AS NEEDED
>
> 2 TABLESPOONS MINCED WHITE ONION
>
> 2 TABLESPOONS MINCED FRESH CILANTRO
>
> TORTILLA CHIPS, FOR SERVING

Over an open flame or in a hot dry skillet, toast the jalapeños until the skins are nicely charred and the chiles are cooked through. Allow to cool. Remove and discard the stems, skins, and seeds. Finely mince or mash the chile.

Combine the Velveeta, cheddar, and half-and-half in a heavy pot. Heat over a low flame, stirring frequently, until the cheeses are fully melted and the sauce is creamy. The sauce will scorch if not frequently stirred. If the mixture becomes too thick, add additional half-and-half.

Remove from the heat. Add the jalapeños, onion, and cilantro. Mix well and transfer to a heated serving bowl.

Serve with crisply fried tortilla chips.

Chef John Folse
Bittersweet Plantation (Donaldsonville, La.)
OLD-FASHIONED MACARONI
AND CHEESE WITH CRAWFISH

SERVES 8

Where better to get yet another benchmark macaroni and cheese recipe than from John Folse in Baton Rouge? I usually don't go for extras and add-ons (I'm not a fan of tomatoes in the mix, for example), but I have found that if you don't overcook it, luscious shellfish can make a hearty indulgence. Crawfish is the perfect seasonal and regional partner that can make this dish feel more like a new classic and less like simply showing off.

ONE 12-OUNCE PACKAGE PENNE

3 TABLESPOONS BUTTER, SOFTENED

1 POUND PEELED CRAWFISH TAILS
   (THAWED IF FROZEN)

2 CUPS GRATED MILD CHEDDAR CHEESE

3 LARGE EGGS

2 CUPS MILK

1/4 TEASPOON PAPRIKA

1/4 TEASPOON CAYENNE PEPPER

SALT AND FRESHLY GROUND BLACK PEPPER

1/2 CUP FRESH BREAD CRUMBS

Preheat the oven to 350°F. Bring a large pot of salted water to a boil.

Cook the macaroni according to the package directions (use the least cooking time suggested, as it will cook further). Butter a 13 by 9-inch baking dish with 1 tablespoon of the butter. When the macaroni is done, drain well and pour into the baking dish. Layer the crawfish on the macaroni, and 1½ cups of the cheese on top of the crawfish.

Beat together the eggs, milk, paprika, cayenne, and salt and pepper to taste. Pour evenly into the baking dish. Sprinkle with the bread crumbs, dot with the remaining 2 tablespoons butter, and top with the remaining ½ cup cheese. Bake for 25 to 30 minutes, until a knife inserted in the center comes out clean. Let sit for a few minutes before serving.

Chef Caroline McDaniel

SHRIMP AND GRITS

SERVES 4

I've known Caroline McDaniel since she was first in her class at La Varenne, École de Cuisine, in Paris, and I was visiting to lecture on "careers in food" to the folks who had paid a lot to work hard and get messy. She's been in New York so long that I often forget she's originally from Miami, Florida, has lived in Winston-Salem, and knows her grits. Here's a tasty recipe that reminds us that a mild or medium cheddar can be the right choice, especially when sweet corn (you know, corn grits) is involved.

- 1 POUND MEDIUM SHRIMP
- 1 TABLESPOON CHOPPED FRESH ROSEMARY
- 1 TABLESPOON CHOPPED FRESH THYME
- 1 CLOVE GARLIC, CHOPPED FINE
- 1 TABLESPOON EXTRA VIRGIN OLIVE OIL
- SALT AND FRESHLY GROUND BLACK PEPPER
- 8 OUNCES THICK-SLICED BACON, CUT INTO ½-INCH PIECES
- 2 CUPS CHICKEN STOCK
- 1 MEDIUM VIDALIA ONION, CUT INTO ½-INCH DICE
- 1 MEDIUM RED BELL PEPPER, CUT INTO ½-INCH DICE
- ½ CUP GRITS, LIKE BOB'S RED MILL (DO NOT USE INSTANT)
- 1 CUP DRY VERMOUTH
- 3 OUNCES WHITE CHEDDAR CHEESE, SHREDDED

Clean and devein the shrimp, then rinse and drain very well; toss in a bowl with a couple of paper towels to remove any excess moisture. Discard the paper towels and add the rosemary, thyme, garlic, and oil, and add pepper to taste. Toss well to coat the shrimp. Cover with plastic wrap, pressing down onto the shrimp and the sides of the bowl; this helps ensure that the shrimp on top get fully marinated. Refrigerate for at least 1 hour and up to 6 hours.

Cook the bacon until just crisp, remove from the pan with a slotted spoon, and drain on paper towels. Pour off all but 1 tablespoon of the bacon grease. (Don't wipe out the pan.)

What happens next will use all your hands and attention, so have everything ready 15 minutes before you plan to serve.

Take the shrimp out of the refrigerator. Heat the chicken stock to boiling in a 1-quart saucepan.

Meanwhile, sauté the onion and red pepper with a pinch of salt and pepper over high heat in the pan with the reserved bacon grease. When the onion starts to brown, scoop out the onion and pepper with a slotted spoon and set aside. Reduce the heat to low under the empty pan.

When the stock is boiling, add the grits in a steady stream, whisking constantly until all of it has been added and it returns to a boil. Reduce the heat to medium-low and give it a good stir with a whisk every couple of minutes.

Raise the heat under the pan to medium and sauté half the shrimp, cooking them about 45 seconds per side. (They'll be pink on the sides but not quite cooked in the middle.) Add them to the onion and pepper. (Stir the grits.) Sauté the remaining shrimp, then add to the vegetables. Add the vermouth to the pan to deglaze; bring to a boil. Add the shrimp mixture and bacon to the pan, reduce the heat, and simmer for 5 minutes.

Meanwhile, the grits should have been stirred several times and should be neither watery loose nor gluey thick. Remove the grits from the heat and stir in the cheddar, 1 teaspoon salt, and ¼ teaspoon black pepper. Make sure you whisk until the cheese is completely melted.

Pour the grits onto a platter and make a well in the center. Spoon the shrimp mixture into the middle and add as much liquid as will fit. Or just serve the grits and shrimp in two separate bowls.

Chef Jan Birnbaum

OVEN-ROASTED RACLETTE WITH SAUSAGE, POTATOES, AND PICKLED GREEN TOMATOES

SERVES 4

Jan Birnbaum is a wonderful cook. He had Catahoula Restaurant & Saloon in California for more than a decade and still has Sazerac, in Seattle, and the recently opened Epic Roasthouse right on the Embarcadero in San Francisco, but his heart, and a lot of his style, comes from his early years in the Big Easy. This recipe is similar to the man: big flavors, easy preparation, and plenty of lovable ingredients.

Traditionally, the rich and sometimes heady raclette is placed in the opening of a wood-fired oven to soften. The molten cheese is then scraped off and served with sausages, potatoes, cornichons, and the like.

Having grown up in the Deep South, Jan knows a lot about pickled green tomatoes. Tomatoes grow so well in the rich alluvial soil of the Mississippi Delta plain that the season is a long and delicious one in and around New Orleans. The large crop led to the tradition of fried and pickled green tomatoes. These tart pickles seem a natural match in place of the cornichons of France.

8 TO 10 OUNCES RACLETTE CHEESE

1 POUND YUKON GOLD, FINGERLING, OR YOUR
FAVORITE SMALL BOILING POTATOES

4 TO 6 LINKS YOUR FAVORITE FULLY-COOKED
SAUSAGE

1 LOAF YOUR FAVORITE CRUSTY DARK BREAD, SLICED

10 OR MORE PIECES CORNICHONS, PICKLED
VEGETABLES, OR SPICY GREEN TOMATO PICKLES
(PAGE 137)

½ CUP GRAINY MUSTARD

Preheat the oven to 250°F. Bring a pot of salted water to a boil.

Soften the cheese in a baking dish in the oven for 25 minutes.

Meanwhile, simmer the potatoes for 15 to 20 minutes, until soft
when poked with a skewer. Drain and set aside, keeping warm.

Slice the sausages thickly on the bias and roast in a heavy pan for
5 to 8 minutes, until heated through. Add the potatoes and let
them brown in the goodness of the sausage.

Toast the bread, preferably on a grill.

To serve, place the cheese at the head of a large, heated platter.
Arrange the sausage slices and potatoes around it. Pile the pickles
to one side and place the mustard next to them. Serve immediately,
with the toast on the side.

American Cheeses

SPICY GREEN TOMATO PICKLES

3 CUPS CIDER VINEGAR

¾ CUP KOSHER SALT

1 ¼ CUPS SUGAR

1 TABLESPOON CELERY SEEDS

¼ CUP WHOLE MUSTARD SEEDS

2 TEASPOONS GROUND TURMERIC

1 TABLESPOON GROUND WHITE PEPPER

8 CLOVES GARLIC, PEELED AND SMASHED

2 TABLESPOONS RED PEPPER FLAKES

2 ½ POUNDS FIRM GREEN TOMATOES,
    CUT INTO 1-INCH CUBES

Combine the vinegar, salt, sugar, celery and mustard seeds, turmeric, white pepper, garlic, and red pepper with 6 cups water in a large stainless steel pot and bring to a boil. Remove from the heat and pour over the tomatoes in a heatproof container. Cool in an ice bath. Store covered in the refrigerator for at least 5 days before using.

NOTE: This makes way more pickles than you'll need for the raclette recipe, but they're well worth the waiting time, and you can enjoy them with other dishes.

Pablo Solanet, FireFly Farms (Bittinger, Md.)

CRAB, FENNEL, AND ALLEGHENY CHÈVRE TART

SERVES 8

Goat cheese and fennel make a wonderful tart; add to that fresh crab and you have something French gone to the Chesapeake Bay.

The recipe makes 2.

Tart Crust

- 16 TABLESPOONS (2 STICKS) COLD UNSALTED BUTTER, CUT INTO SMALL CUBES, PLUS EXTRA FOR THE PANS
- 4 CUPS ALL-PURPOSE FLOUR, PLUS EXTRA FOR ROLLING
- 1 TABLESPOON SALT
- 1 CUP ICE WATER

Filling

- 8 TABLESPOONS (1 STICK) UNSALTED BUTTER
- 1½ POUNDS ONIONS, FINELY CHOPPED
- 8 OUNCES LEEKS, WHITE PART ONLY, THINLY SLICED
- 8 OUNCES FENNEL, THINLY SLICED
- SALT AND FRESHLY GROUND BLACK PEPPER
- ONE 9-OUNCE LOG ALLEGHENY CHÈVRE FROM FIREFLY FARMS OR OTHER SOFT FRESH GOAT CHEESE
- 2 LARGE EGGS, LIGHTLY BEATEN
- 1 CUP HEAVY CREAM
- ½ CUP GRATED PARMESAN CHEESE
- 1 TABLESPOON GRATED LEMON ZEST
- ½ CUP FINELY CHOPPED FRESH CHIVES
- ¼ CUP FINELY CHOPPED FRESH TARRAGON
- ½ TEASPOON CAYENNE PEPPER
- ½ TEASPOON FRESHLY GRATED NUTMEG
- 1 POUND CRABMEAT, PICKED OVER

To make the tart crust, butter two 10-inch tart pans with removable bottoms. Set aside in the refrigerator.

In a food processor fitted with the metal blade, combine the flour and salt. Add the cubed butter and pulse to combine until the mixture resembles a coarse meal. Pea-size bits of butter should be visible throughout the flour. With the processor running, slowly add the water until dough forms around the blade. Remove from the processor, shape into a disk, and wrap in plastic wrap. Chill for at least 30 minutes.

Meanwhile, preheat the oven to 375°F.

Divide the dough in half. On a floured surface, roll out each half of the dough in a 12-inch round. Fit the dough into the tart pans and trim the excess. Line each with a parchment paper round and fill with pie weights. Chill for 15 minutes. Bake for 15 minutes. Remove the pie weights and parchment paper and bake for 15 minutes more. Remove from the oven and set aside to cool. Turn the oven down to 350°F.

To make the filling, melt the butter in a large heavy-bottomed skillet. Add the onions, leeks, and fennel. Season with salt and pepper. Cook for about 15 minutes, stirring frequently, until softened and slightly browned. Remove from the heat.

In a medium bowl, combine the goat cheese, eggs, cream, Parmesan, lemon zest, chives, tarragon, cayenne, nutmeg, and cooked vegetables. Season with salt and pepper. Gently fold in the crabmeat until combined.

Divide the filling between the tart shells, spreading it evenly. Bake until set, 35 to 40 minutes. Serve warm.

Chef Scott Peacock,
from The Gift of Southern Cooking
A Perfect Pimento Cheese

MAKES ABOUT 2 CUPS

Nothing says southern like pimento cheese and nobody more beautifully embodies and deftly offers the tastes of the South than Scott Peacock of Watershed Restaurant in Decatur, Georgia. This classic recipe comes from his *The Gift of Southern Cooking* from Knopf, written with the legendary Edna Lewis.

2 ½ CUPS (10 OUNCES) GRATED EXTRA SHARP
    CHEDDAR CHEESE

⅛ TEASPOON CAYENNE PEPPER, OR TO TASTE

¾ CUP HOMEMADE MAYONNAISE (PAGE 141)

3 TABLESPOONS FINELY CHOPPED ROASTED RED
    BELL PEPPER OR PIMENTO (SEE NOTE)

SALT, IF NEEDED

5 OR 6 GRINDS BLACK PEPPER

Stir together all of the ingredients in a mixing bowl until they are well mixed and creamy. Taste carefully for seasoning and adjust as needed. Cover and store, refrigerated, until ready to use.

A Note on Roasting and Peeling Peppers

There is more than one way to roast peppers, but the way we find easiest is this: Wash and dry the peppers you are going to roast, then rub the exterior of each pepper with a very small amount of vegetable or olive oil—less than a teaspoon per pepper. Put the oiled peppers into a baking dish, and bake in a preheated 425°F oven for 20 minutes. The pepper will look charred in patches and be blistered all over. Remove from the oven, and transfer the peppers to a bowl that can be tightly covered. Cover and let rest until the peppers are cool enough to handle. Once they are cooled, with a paring knife peel off the outer skin from the peppers, remove the stem, cut open, and remove the seeds as well. Resist the urge to rinse under water to clean the peppers perfectly. It is preferable to have an occasional seed or a bit of charred pepper than to wash away the delicious pepper flavor. Roasted and peeled peppers can be kept refrigerated for 2 or 3 days before using.

MAYONNAISE

MAKES ABOUT 1¾ CUPS

I TABLESPOON CIDER VINEGAR

I TABLESPOON FRESHLY SQUEEZED LEMON JUICE

I TEASPOON SEA SALT

I TEASPOON DRY MUSTARD

2 LARGE EGG YOLKS

1½ CUPS VEGETABLE OIL OR LIGHT OLIVE OIL,
  OR A COMBINATION

I TABLESPOON HOT WATER

Put the vinegar, lemon juice, salt, and mustard into a bowl, and whisk or stir until the salt and mustard are dissolved. Add the egg yolks and beat until smooth. Add the oil, drop by drop at first, and then in a slow, steady stream, whisking or stirring constantly until all of the oil has been incorporated and you have a very thick emulsion. Stir in the hot water until smooth. Refrigerated, homemade mayonnaise will keep for up to 1 week.

Paula Lambert's

LEMON–GOAT CHEESE TART

SERVES 8

I just love a woman with a tart crust. This addictive dessert combines all the best qualities of tart, sour, zippy, and sweet (which sounds like Willie Wonka's law firm). For a slightly milder and more aromatic version, use Meyer lemons and garnish with candied peel or just the zest of that fruit.

Tart Crust

- 1¼ CUPS UNBLEACHED ALL-PURPOSE FLOUR
- ¼ CUP CONFECTIONERS' SUGAR
- 10 TABLESPOONS (1¼ STICKS) UNSALTED BUTTER

Filling

- ½ CUP GOAT CHEESE (4 OUNCES)
- ½ CUP CRÈME FRAÎCHE OR SOUR CREAM (4 OUNCES)
- ¼ CUP SUGAR
- 1 LARGE EGG
- 2½ TEASPOONS UNBLEACHED ALL-PURPOSE FLOUR

Lemon Curd

- 6 LARGE EGG YOLKS
- ½ CUP FRESHLY SQUEEZED LEMON JUICE
- 1 CUP GRANULATED SUGAR
- 4 TABLESPOONS (½ STICK) UNSALTED BUTTER
- 2 TABLESPOONS CONFECTIONERS' SUGAR, FOR GARNISH (OPTIONAL)

For the tart crust, preheat the oven to 350°F.

Combine the flour, sugar, and butter in a food processor fitted with the steel blade. Pulse until a soft ball begins to form on the blade. Be careful not to overprocess. Remove the dough and press into the bottom and up the sides of an 11-inch tart pan with a removable bottom. Prick the dough with a fork and refrigerate for 30 minutes.

Bake for 15 to 20 minutes, until golden brown. Remove from the oven and set aside and let cool. Leave the oven on.

For the filling, mix the goat cheese, crème fraîche, sugar, egg, and flour together in a small bowl. Pour into the tart crust. Bake for 20 to 25 minutes, until the filling is just set. Set aside on a wire rack to cool.

For the lemon curd, combine the egg yolks, lemon juice, and granulated sugar in the top of a double boiler over simmering water. Cook over medium-low heat, stirring frequently, until the mixture coats the back of a spoon, about 10 minutes. Do not boil. When the mixture thickens and wisps of steam start to rise from it, remove from the heat and stir in the butter until it melts. Set aside to cool for 15 minutes. Pour the lemon curd over the baked tart. Refrigerate for at least 1 hour and up to 12 hours before serving.

Just before serving, if desired, sprinkle the chilled tart with the confectioners' sugar, making an even layer. Holding a propane torch 4 to 5 inches away, heat the sugar until it turns golden brown and caramelizes. Alternatively, preheat the broiler to high and place the tart 3 inches below the heat.

To serve, slice into wedges. Serve chilled.

Others to Look For

There are a lot of little cheesemakers all over the South, many of whom make lovely fresh and ripened goat cheeses that don't travel far from home.

Elizabeth Parnell of **Fromagerie Belle Chèvre** in Elkmont, Alabama, started making goat cheese in 1989 at the age of fifty-eight. Her handcrafted farmstead cheese has been served to international leaders at White House dinners and to a lot of happy locals. Recently she passed the business and her beloved creamery into the hands of Tasia Malakasis, to whom she taught cheesemaking.

Donna Doel makes award-winning goat cheese from her sixteen-acre **Doeling Dairy Goat Farm** in Fayetteville, Arkansas. Her desire to make cheese was born out of a sustainable approach to farming and food production, not to mention trips to France. Her fresh chèvre is solid.

The Feete family of **Meadow Creek Dairy** in Virginia produces mild and creamy Appalachian table cheese from the milk of their Jersey cows, among other varieties.

Traders Point Creamery makes ice cream and American Cheese Society award-winning yogurt, as well as fresh and aged cheeses.

I'd include **Goat Lady Dairy** for the town name alone. They make a broad range of cheeses that continue to get better.

Fromagerie Belle Chèvre
26910 Bethel Road
Elkmont, AL 35620
Tel.: 800-735-2238
www.bellechevre.com

Doeling Dairy Goat Farm
2877 South Leo Ammons Road
Fayetteville, AR 72701
Tel.: 888-524-4571
www.doelingdairy.com

Meadow Creek Dairy
6724 Meadow Creek Road
Galax, VA 24333
Tel.: 888-236-0622
Fax: 276-236-4955
www.meadowcreekdairy.com

Traders Point Creamery
9101 Moore Road
Zionsville, IN 46077
Tel.: 317-733-1700
www.tpforganics.com

Goat Lady Dairy
3515 Jess Hackett Road
Climax, NC 27233
Tel.: 336-824-2163
www.goatladydairy.com

The South

The Middle West

I was a waiter on a train that ran between Oakland, California, and downtown Chicago. The *California Zephyr* made the trip in just under two and a half days. We'd serve nearly six hundred people in forty-eight seats in two hours flat, at ninety miles an hour.

We'd bounce into what was then the biggest city I'd ever seen. Buildings so high, and yet streets so clean. People were a polite kind of friendly I'd never experienced. It was the land of Mies van der Rohe designs and the Wrigley Building, towering black monoliths and the Marshall Field department store, with its legendary melting Frango mints.

My coworkers bolted the crew car and disappeared into the night. I checked into my tiny single room, changed out of my monkey suit into Sunday best, and went to dinner using all my tips from several journeys, to the legendary Pump Room or the Coq d'Or at the Drake Hotel. In the morning I'd get up in time to marvel at the Art Institute or go into what felt like an actual coal mine in a museum.

Cheese was not a Second City mainstay, except in deep-dish pizza or melted over nearly any sandwich.

But the American Midwest is well known for its cheeses, which have traditionally come mostly from Wisconsin. The largest cheese producer (so far) and second in dairy production only to California, "America's Dairyland" has been known to make any kind of anyone else's cheese, with an emphasis on the central and northern European traditions familiar to many of its original settlers. To many in the middle of the country, post–World War II, cheese (like Limburger) was cheap protein and an American birthright.

In fact, the Midwest is where goat's milk products first established major acceptance. It was at the World's Fair in 1904 in St. Louis, Missouri, that America held our first goat dairy show.

These days, Wisconsin's new artisan cheesemakers are finally joining the big producers. But even in the midst of the ever-careful expansion, there are a few old favorites, and some real sleepers that cheese lovers should be careful not to overlook. In a state where more than 90 percent of the milk becomes cheese, where all cheesemakers must have state certification, and where the big European companies first found a North American foothold, there's still plenty of room for innovation and creativity.

Mike Gingrich
Uplands Cheese Company

It was one of those "Ah-ha!" moments, at a hotel reception
for the American Cheese Society in Louisville, Kentucky. I was
ambling past the Wisconsin table and grabbed a small hunk of
something I hadn't tasted before. Pleasant Ridge Reserve seemed
to be a title of appealing pretension, more like a cult red wine
than a farmstead cheese.

The year was 2001 and the cheese went on to win Best
of Show in highly competitive judging. Four years later the
ACS was back in Louisville, and Pleasant Ridge Reserve from
the Uplands Cheese Company in Wisconsin was again the
big winner.

This extraordinary ten-pound wheel is made in the style of
French Alpine wheels such as ones most often called Gruyère. It
is a firm, washed-rind, aged cheese made from the very seasonal
unpasteurized milk of cows raised in open fields of sweet grass,
wildflowers, clovers, and herbs.

Mike Gingrich is married to his childhood sweetheart,
Carol. He once worked for Xerox, but his mother's family had
been in dairy farming for years. The couple came to feel that
a farm was the perfect place to raise kids, so with friends Don
and Jeanne Patenaude, they set up on 300 acres forty miles west
of Madison.

Uplands Cheese Company, Inc.

5023 State Road 23 North

Dodgeville, WI 53533

Tel.: 888-935-5558

Fax: 608-935-7030

www.uplandscheese.com

contact@uplandscheese.com

CHEESE:

Pleasant Ridge Reserve

American Cheeses

CHEESEMAKER:

Auricchio

Some of the more successful cheese companies in the United
States are related to European family businesses or international
conglomerates. The folks in Wisconsin have been thrilled every
time their milk gets chosen by some dairy titan. Some make good
cheese; some just fill shelves.

Auricchio provolone is one of the good ones. A secret of the
company's success, dating back to its origin near Naples, Italy, in
1877, is its specially developed rennet, called the "secret of Don
Gennaro," for Gennaro Auricchio, who founded the company.

Aurricchio

3018 Helsan Drive

PO Box 282

Richfield, WI 53076

Tel.: 800-782-0741

Fax: 262-677-3806

www.dcicheeseco.com

CHEESES:

Parmesan

Provolone

Mozzarella

Stella Cheese Company

I love artisan cheeses and the folks who make them. So why am I writing about a good-sized industrial cheese company that supplies grocery stores everywhere? Because if you go into a lot of good cheese shops or cheese departments at better groceries, you'll often see a brown wax-covered wheel called Medium Asiago.

It's not from a small town in Italy. It's from a big factory (or two) in Wisconsin. And it's not exactly the creamy, lively, slightly sour cheese (Asiago fresco is a real delight) made in Italy. It's a nutty, sweet, mellow, and fairly firm grating cheese that is unique and a real addition to any collection, particularly for anyone who wants to cook with good ingredients at reasonably affordable prices.

Stella Cheese Company
www.stellacheese.com

CHEESES:

Medium Asiago

Romano

Parmesan

Parmesan and Romano Blend

Fontinella

Three-Cheese Italian Blend

Italian Sharp

Kasseri

Blue

Feta

Gorgonzola

Mary and Dave Falk
Love Tree Farm

Just about a year before the stock market crashed in 1987,
Mary and Dave Falk were busy building a life in the magnificent
countryside of northern Wisconsin.

Under the radar of what most people think of as big
industrial midwestern cheesemaking, they tended their flocks on
130 acres of grazing land, while the other 70 acres stayed free as a
wildlife habitat. These are folks in sync with nature.

Early in the twenty-first century, they began a stunning
sweep of award winning, honoring nearly every sort of young
sheep's milk cheese they decided to make. I particularly love their
"Holmes" series, Big and Little, with their unique coating of herbs
and nettles. They call it a "wake-up call for the taste buds." I call it
a midcontinent treasure.

LoveTree Farmstead Cheese
12413 County Road Z
Grantsburg, WI 54840
Tel.: 715-488-2966
Fax: 715-488-3957
www.lovetreefarmstead.com
maryf@lovetreefarm.com

CHEESES:

RAW MILK

Gabrielson Lake (cow's milk)

Trade Lake Cedar (sheep's milk)

CAVE AGED

Sumac Holmes

Big Holmes

LoveTree's Little Holmes

LoveTree's Cubs

LoveTree's Black Bears

American Cheeses

CHEESEMAKER:

Carr Valley Cheese Company

Wisconsin does have a white cheddar that is cloth wrapped (or bandaged, as it's called in the cheese world) and aged in caves. It's from the hundred-year-old Carr Valley Cheese Company and, at this writing, the only one of its kind in the state.

Made in eleven-pound wheels, it's on proud display in their shops—three of the four are factories with retail outlets. I'm happy about the popularity and acclaim this cheese has gotten, because, after a century, it's nice to see this family-owned company comfortably moving ahead in some more classical directions.

Their Colby is a good take on that squeaky-clean cheese, and they have a wonderful Virgin-Pine Native Sheep Blue that's extraordinary (as in *good*).

Carr Valley Cheese Company, Inc.
S3797 County Road G
La Valle, WI 53941
Tel.: 800-462-7258
Fax: 608-986-2906
www.carrvalleycheese.com

CHEESES:

Colby	*Mild Cheddar*
Fresh Cheddar Curd	*Medium Cheddar*
Baby Cheddar	*Aged Cheddar (one to six years)*

155

The Middle West

Apple-Smoked Cheddar

Beer Cheddar

Garlic Cheddar

Hickory-Smoked Cheddar

Horseradish Cheddar

Mammoth Cheddar

Airco

Benedictine

Bessie's Blend

Canaria

Caso Bolo Mellage

Cave Aged Mellage

Gran Canaria

Mellage

Menage

Mobay

Goat Feta

Shepherd's Blend

Cranberry Cheddar

Creama Kasa

Double Gloucester

Feta

Gouda

Smoked Gouda

Havarti

Cave Aged Marisa

Marisa

River Bend Sheep

Virgin-Pine Native Sheep Blue

Nannie Eye Reserve

Smoked Nannie Eye Reserve

Monterey Jack

Monastery

Port Salue

Tom's Swiss

Vintage Van Gogh

Virgin-Pine Native Blue

Goat Cheddar

Swedish Farmers

Ba Ba Blue

Baraboo Blue

Snow White Goat Cheddar

Chèvre au Lait

Billy Blue

Cardona

Aged Cardona

Cocoa Cardona

CHEESEMAKER:
Widmer's Cheese Cellars

This is a classic midwestern story: An industrious Swiss immigrant settles in Wisconsin and starts making cheese. Eventually, while known for several good varieties, it is the well-aged yellow cheddar that is the standard bearer for this all-American family business.

Even back in the 1970s, it seemed clear that Wisconsin cheddar—usually the orange sort, colored by the tasteless powder of finely ground annatto seeds—only got really interesting after about four years. Young, it's perfectly pleasant but so mild that, while useful, it's hardly memorable.

For a while, as in other parts of the country, it was just not profitable to keep these cheeses around long enough to age into something special, so I generally ignored them. With a renewed and deeper interest in cheese sweeping the country, this variety became worth a second look. Widmer's very good aged cheddar is just such a cheese.

Widmer's Cheese Cellars
214 West Henni Street
PO Box 127
Theresa, WI 53091
Tel.: 888-878-1107
Fax: 920-488-2130
www.widmerscheese.com
info@widmerscheese.com

CHEESES:

Pepper Cheddar Curds

Brick Curds

Cheddar Curds

Pepper Cheddar

Cheddar (aged one, two, four, or six years)

Mild Cheddar

Vegetable Colby

Pepper Colby

Caraway Colby

Colby

Aged Brick

Mild Specialty Brick

Pepper Brick

Jalapeño Pepper Brick

Jalapeño Pepper Cheddar

CHEESEMAKER:

Myron Olson
Chalet Cheese Cooperative

This wonderful all-American cheese company is the last to make good old stinky Limburger. Personally, I think this cheese has an inferiority complex it needs to lose. I told their wonderful head cheesemaker, Myron Olson, they ought to make up special batches, wrap them in some fancy paper, call them "select," and sell them for three times the price. He blushed.

Limburger and its late, great Ohio cousin, Liederkranz, were really Depression cheeses, poor man's protein made from the end-of-season leavings, after the big Swiss-style wheels were done and gone. Mostly sold by Kraft since the 1930s, Limburger was a sturdy midwestern staple, on toast for breakfast, on dark rye for lunch, and on potatoes with dinner.

Limburger is a washed-rind cheese, using the same cultures that have been kept alive and working for more than forty years down there in the lonely cellar. It's an exacting science. Olson walks in and takes a sniff. If it's a clean, light smell, he knows all's well. If he detects a little sour something, he knows adjustments are in order, his bag of tricks a closely held secret.

The factory has been there since 1885. The machinery for cutting, wrapping, packing, and all, was made and installed about 1937. The place was dubbed the World's Most Modern Limburger Cheese Factory in 1947. As with many dairy workers, especially in the Midwest, Myron came to work in 1970 right out of high school, worked through college (where he studied agriculture economics), and became a cheesemaker soon after.

There was a break in the 1980s when he went off to "see the world" but was drawn back and became head "boss guy cheesemaker manager" in the early 1990s, just the third one since the 1930s.

We did a vertical tasting of Limburger, then one with very good German Brick. These are sturdy cheeses not to be missed.

Chalet Cheese Cooperative

N4858 Highway N

Monroe, WI 53566

Tel.: 608-325-4343

Fax: 608-325-4409

chalet@cppweb.com

CHEESE:

Limburger	*Brick*
Baby Swiss	*Muenster*
Swiss	*Blue Cheese*
Natural Smoked Swiss	*Butter*
Cheddar	*Fresh Curds*
Havarti	*String Cheese*
German Brick	

CHEESEMAKER:

Roth Käse

Here's another excellent example of how a lot of really good cheese can be made all in one place.

Roth Käse makes a whole lot more cheese—more than 150,000 pounds a week when we visited a few years ago—than we think of as a classical artisan cheesemaker. That's why it came as somewhat of a surprise when their very fine, top-of-the-line Grand Cru Gruyère Surchoix won Best of Show at the American Cheese Society judging just a few years after coming to market. But "best of" it certainly was.

They also make a raw milk, delicious Buttermilk Blue, so named by famed California cheesemaker Ig Vella, along with a host of other specialties, and distribute other folks' cheeses to boot. Just proves that big can be good, too.

Roth Käse
627 Second Street
Monroe, WI 53566
Tel.: 608-328-2122
www.rothkase.com
info@rothkase.com

CHEESES:

Serafina

Knight's Vail

Landhaus St. Bernard's

Landhaus Butterkäse

Landhaus Braukäse

Bambina Fontina

MezzaLuna Gorgonzola

MezzaLuna Fontina

MezzaLuna Fontiago

Van Gogh Smoked Gouda

Vintage Van Gogh

*Donovan's Double
Diamond Darby*

Rocky Top Smoked Cheddar

*Red Spruce Aged Cheddar
(aged four, five, or seven years)*

Gruyère

Buttermilk Blue

Havarti

Havarti with Dill

Havarti with Jalapeño

Havarti with Pesto

*Havarti with Horseradish
and Chives*

Solé GranQueso

Alp and Dell Baby Swiss

Landhause Lace Käse

Rofumo

Krönenost Swedish-Style Fontina

American Cheeses

Mary Basta, The Chocolate Swan (Milwaukee and Las Vegas)

ESCARGOTS WITH ROASTED GARLIC AND GORGONZOLA

SERVES 6

This fairly quick and straightforward recipe seems totally retro and completely modern at the same time. It's simply delicious.

Serve with a spicy pinot noir or a very crisp sauvignon blanc.

1 HEAD GARLIC

¼ CUP EXTRA VIRGIN OLIVE OIL, PLUS EXTRA FOR ROASTING THE GARLIC

SALT

1 TEASPOON FRESHLY GROUND BLACK PEPPER, PLUS EXTRA FOR ROASTING THE GARLIC

8 TABLESPOONS (1 STICK) UNSALTED BUTTER, SOFTENED

30 TO 35 EXTRA LARGE ESCARGOTS

8 OUNCES GORGONZOLA OR MAYTAG BLUE CHEESE

SOURDOUGH TOASTS, FOR SERVING

Preheat the oven to 350°F.

Sprinkle the head of garlic with olive oil, salt, and pepper. Wrap in foil and roast for 45 minutes. Let cool, then squeeze the garlic from each clove into a bowl. Blend the butter with the garlic and the 1 teaspoon pepper. Mix in the ¼ cup olive oil.

Thoroughly rinse the snails under cool water. Drain and place in a baking dish. Melt the garlic butter and pour on top. Sprinkle with the Gorgonzola and bake for 25 minutes, or until the outside begins to bubble and the cheese is thoroughly melted. Serve with toasted sourdough rounds.

Widmer's Cheese Cellars

CHERRY TOMATOES STUFFED WITH WISCONSIN HERBED CHEESE

MAKES 3 DOZEN

I happen to love stuffed cherry tomatoes. They're so 1950s, they make me giggle, but they're really tasty and cherry tomatoes are usually the first tomato of the season to be ripe and sweet, and the last to still hang on.

3 DOZEN ATTRACTIVE CHERRY TOMATOES,
    IDEALLY 1 TO 1½ INCHES IN DIAMETER

2 TABLESPOONS PREPARED BASIL PESTO OR
    3 TABLESPOONS CHOPPED FRESH BASIL LEAVES

1 TEASPOON MINCED GARLIC

2 TABLESPOONS CHOPPED FRESH PARSLEY

2 TABLESPOONS CHOPPED FRESH CHIVES

1 TABLESPOON CHOPPED FRESH TARRAGON OR DILL

10 OUNCES WISCONSIN CREAM CHEESE

36 SMALL FRESH PARSLEY OR DILL SPRIGS,
    FOR GARNISH

With a very sharp paring knife, cut off the top third of each cherry tomato from the stem end. Carefully scoop out the inside of each cherry tomato (a small melon baller works well) and set the tomato aside.

In a food processor fitted with the metal blade, combine the pesto, garlic, chopped parsley, chives, and tarragon, and process for 15 seconds. Add the cream cheese and process for another 30 to 45 seconds, until the filling is free of lumps.

Place the filling in a pastry bag fitted with a star tip and pipe into each cherry tomato. Garnish the tops with a fresh herb sprig. Refrigerate until ready to serve.

Chef Hans Burtscher, Grand Hotel (Mackinac Island, Mich.)

BLUE CHEESE PRALINES

MAKES 12 TO 14 PRALINES

This is a combination of sweet and savory that makes all of the ingredients taste better than they would on their own. Toasting the nuts, reducing the vinegar, blending the two cheeses, and adding gin—just reading the recipe makes me swoon with pleasure. Served with a lightly dressed butter lettuce salad or just paired with cocktails, this is a treat.

Balsamic Syrup

> 2 CUPS BALSAMIC VINEGAR
>
> ⅓ CUP HONEY
>
> 1 TABLESPOON FINELY CHOPPED FRESH THYME

Pralines

> 4 OUNCES BUTTERMILK BLUE CHEESE (FROM ROTH KÄSE)
>
> 14 OUNCES BRIE CHEESE
>
> 4 OUNCES CREAM CHEESE
>
> 1 TABLESPOON GIN
>
> 1 TABLESPOON WHITE BALSAMIC VINEGAR
>
> 2 TABLESPOONS MINCED FRESH CHIVES
>
> SALT AND FRESHLY GROUND BLACK PEPPER
>
> ⅓ CUP FINELY CHOPPED TOASTED PECANS
>
> ⅓ CUP FINELY CHOPPED TOASTED WALNUTS

To make the balsamic syrup, combine the vinegar, honey, and thyme in a sauté pan. Bring to a boil, then reduce the heat and simmer until reduced by three quarters and has a syrup-like consistency. Strain through a fine sieve and set aside.

To make the pralines, combine the blue cheese, Brie, cream cheese, gin, white balsamic vinegar, chives, and salt and pepper to taste in a bowl and beat until smooth. Scoop into 12 to 14 small mounds and place on a plate covered with plastic wrap. Refrigerate until firm, at least 30 minutes.

Combine the pecans and walnuts in a shallow dish. Roll the cheese mounds into balls and coat them evenly with the nuts. Drizzle each praline with balsamic syrup and serve.

Roth Käse

PRIVATE RESERVE FONDUE

SERVES 6

The key to any really good fondue is—not surprisingly—really good cheese with complex flavors and enough zip to stand up to the booze of choice. This recipe is really quite delicious.

A good crusty Italian loaf cut into 1-inch cubes dips nicely in the fondue. Serve with fresh fruit in season and a light, dry wine such as riesling.

- 1 CLOVE GARLIC, HALVED
- 2 CUPS DRY WHITE WINE SUCH AS SAUVIGNON BLANC OR RIESLING
- JUICE OF ½ LEMON, STRAINED
- 2 TABLESPOONS SWISS KIRSCH
- 1 SCANT TABLESPOON CORNSTARCH
- 8 OUNCES MEZZALUNA FONTIAGO, SHREDDED, AT ROOM TEMPERATURE
- 1½ POUNDS 12-MONTH-OLD GRAND CRU GRUYÈRE SURCHOIX, SHREDDED, AT ROOM TEMPERATURE
- FRESHLY GRATED NUTMEG
- FRESHLY GROUND BLACK PEPPER

Rub the inside of a flameproof fondue pot with the garlic. Place over low heat, add the wine, and bring to a low simmer; do not boil. Add the lemon juice and cook for 1 minute. In a small cup, blend the kirsch into the cornstarch. Stir into the mixture in the fondue pot. Stirring constantly, blend in the cheeses. Cook for 2 minutes, stirring, then dust with nutmeg and pepper to taste. Place on the fondue burner and enjoy.

Chef Paul Kahan, Blackbird (Chicago)

PLEASANT RIDGE RESERVE FARMSTEAD CHEESE WITH CRISPY SERRANO HAM, FRISÉE, AND CANDIED HAZELNUTS

SERVES 8 AS AN APPETIZER, 4 AS A MAIN COURSE

This is the sort of dish that could be used as a tapa or small plate, a salad, or expanded into a main course. It's all about the flavors, freshness, and quality of the ingredients.

Candied Hazelnuts

    I TEASPOON GRAPESEED OIL

    ¼ CUP SUGAR

    I CUP SKINNED HAZELNUTS

    SALT

Crispy Serrano Ham

    ¼ CUP SUGAR

    8 PAPER-THIN SLICES SERRANO HAM

Dressing

    ½ SMALL SHALLOT, MINCED

    I TEASPOON FRESH THYME LEAVES

    ½ TEASPOON GRAINY MUSTARD

    8 BLACK PEPPERCORNS, CRUSHED

    2 TABLESPOONS SHERRY VINEGAR

    6 TABLESPOONS HAZELNUT OIL

    SALT

Salad and Finishing

1 BULB FENNEL

1 HEAD FRISÉE, WHITE PART ONLY

1 BUNCH WATERCRESS, HEAVY STEMS REMOVED

8 CHIVES, SNIPPED INTO 1-INCH LENGTHS

2 RIPE FORELLE PEARS, OR OTHER RIPE, FIRM PEAR, PREFERABLY RED-SKINNED

8 OUNCES PLEASANT RIDGE RESERVE CHEESE (FROM UPLANDS CHEESE COMPANY), SHAVED INTO 8 PIECES

To make the candied hazelnuts, heat the grapeseed oil in a sauté pan over medium-high heat. Add the sugar and let it melt completely. Add the hazelnuts and stir to coat. Season with salt. Spread out on a plate and let cool to room temperature. Store in a tightly covered container.

To make the crispy Serrano ham, preheat the oven to 250°F. In a small saucepan, combine the sugar with ¼ cup water. Bring to a boil, stirring until all the sugar has dissolved. Let cool to room temperature.

Cover a baking sheet with parchment paper. Place the ham on the baking sheet in a single layer. Brush the syrup over the ham. Lay another piece of parchment paper over the ham. Place a second baking sheet on top of the parchment and weight it down with a heavy ovenproof object. Bake for 30 to 40 minutes, until crisp. Uncover, let cool, and store in a tightly covered container.

American Cheeses

To make the dressing, place the shallot, thyme, mustard, peppercorns, and sherry vinegar in a small bowl. Whisk vigorously. Slowly drizzle in the oil, whisking until incorporated. Taste the dressing and season with salt. It should be acidic, though you may add more oil if necessary.

To make the salad, cut the fennel bulb into quarters. Cut out the core and slice the fennel as thin as possible. Place in a large bowl. Separate the frisée and add to the fennel. Add the watercress, chives, and ¼ cup of the candied hazelnuts. Core the pears, slice lengthwise as thin as possible, and add to the salad. Drizzle with the dressing and toss gently to combine.

Place 1 slice of crispy Serrano ham on each plate. Top with a slice of cheese. Top with salad and serve immediately.

Amy Myrdal's

FARM GIRL QUICHE

SERVES 6 TO 8

"Who has time to make piecrust when the cows need milking, the garden needs weeding, and the laundry needs to be taken in before the next thunderstorm? This recipe is similar to a quiche Lorraine, but it's much easier to make," says our friend Amy Myrdal, a genuine North Dakota girl who now works in California. A tomato and avocado salad is a nice accompaniment.

1 POUND BACON

8 LARGE EGGS, BEATEN

3 CUPS WHOLE OR 2% MILK

1 TEASPOON PREPARED MUSTARD

2 TABLESPOONS GRATED WHITE OR YELLOW ONION

3 TABLESPOONS CHOPPED FRESH CHIVES

1 TEASPOON SALT

1 TEASPOON FRESHLY GROUND BLACK PEPPER

ONE 10-OUNCE PACKAGE FROZEN CHOPPED SPINACH, THAWED, DRAINED, AND SQUEEZED DRY

6 CUPS CUBED FRENCH OR ITALIAN BREAD

2 CUPS GRATED MEDIUM CHEDDAR CHEESE, 2 YEARS OLD OR YOUNGER

½ CUP FRESHLY GRATED ASIAGO

Preheat the oven to 325°F.

Cook the bacon until crisp. Set on paper towels to drain, and when cool, crumble into bits. In a large mixing bowl combine the eggs, milk, mustard, grated onion, chives, salt, and pepper. Add the spinach, bread cubes, and bacon and toss well.

Transfer the mixture to a 13 by 9-inch baking dish. Top with the cheddar and asiago cheese and bake for 1 hour. Serve warm or cold.

Zingerman's Roadhouse (Ann Arbor, Mich.)

MACARONI AND THREE-PEPPERCORN GOAT CHEESE

SERVES 4

I love that our recipe for midwestern mac and cheese uses handmade goat cheese. My, how the world has changed. This landmark deli (and now Roadhouse and Creamery and mail-order house) in an old building by the local farmer's market has been gathering great foods from around the world, and down the road, for two dozen years.

At Zingerman's Roadhouse, they serve this dish with a fried round of the Creamery's Aged Chelsea, a mold-ripened little goat log we just love atop the mac.

Macaroni and Cheese

COARSE SEA SALT

1 POUND MACARONI, PREFERABLY MARTELLI

2 TABLESPOONS BUTTER

¼ CUP DICED ONION

1 BAY LEAF

2 TABLESPOONS ALL-PURPOSE FLOUR

1½ CUPS MILK

¼ CUP HEAVY CREAM

1 TEASPOON DIJON MUSTARD

2 CUPS ZINGERMAN'S CREAMERY FRESH GOAT CHEESE (ABOUT 1 POUND)

¾ CUP CHOPPED ROASTED RED PEPPERS

2 TEASPOONS FRESHLY GROUND BLACK PEPPER, PLUS MORE TO TASTE

1 TEASPOON FRESHLY GROUND WHITE PEPPER

1 TEASPOON FRESHLY GROUND GREEN PEPPERCORNS

Aged Chelsea

  1 LARGE EGG

  2 TABLESPOONS MILK

  1 TABLESPOON BUTTER

  4 OUNCES ZINGERMAN'S CREAMERY AGED CHELSEA,
  CUT INTO 4 ROUNDS

  1 CUP BREAD CRUMBS (FRESH OR DRIED)

Bring a large pot of water to a boil. Add 1 to 2 tablespoons salt and the pasta and stir well. Cook for about 13 minutes (if using Martelli), until the pasta is al dente. Drain and set aside.

Meanwhile, melt the butter in a large heavy-bottomed pot over medium-high heat. Add the onion and bay leaf and sauté until the onion is soft, about 5 minutes. Remove the bay leaf. Stir in the flour, and cook for about 1 minute, stirring constantly. Slowly add the milk, a little at a time, stirring constantly to avoid lumping. When the flour and milk have been completely combined, stir in the cream. Keep the mixture at a gentle simmer (not at a high boil) until it thickens, 2 to 3 minutes.

Reduce the heat to medium. Stir in the mustard, goat cheese, red peppers, ground pepper, and salt to taste.

Stir the pasta into the sauce. Taste and adjust the seasoning if necessary. Cover and remove from the heat.

To fry the Chelseas, combine the egg and milk in a small bowl. Melt the butter over moderately high heat in a heavy-bottomed skillet. Coat each cheese round with the egg wash, then completely coat in bread crumbs. Fry the cheese for about 1 minute on each side, until golden.

Divide the macaroni and sauce among four bowls. Top each bowl with a golden Aged Chelsea. Dig in!

Joe Castro's *(Capriol Farmstead)*

Kentucky Spoon Bread with Goat Cheese and Country Ham

SERVES 4 TO 6

Building on my own personal belief that pork of any sort, especially ham or bacon, is an essential food group, I was delighted to discover another excuse to mix it with other favorite ingredients like leeks and tasty, fresh goat cheese.

American Cheeses

- 8 TABLESPOONS (1 STICK) BUTTER, PLUS EXTRA FOR THE CASSEROLE
- 2 LEEKS, CLEANED, WHITE PARTS ONLY, THINLY SLICED
- 2½ CUPS MILK
- 2 CUPS HALF-AND-HALF
- 1 TABLESPOON SUGAR
- 1 CUP CORNMEAL
- ½ CUP ALL-PURPOSE FLOUR
- 6 LARGE EGGS, SEPARATED
- ¼ CUP HEAVY CREAM
- ½ CUP CRUMBLED FRESH GOAT CHEESE
- ¼ CUP DICED COUNTRY HAM OR PROSCIUTTO
- SORGHUM SYRUP, FOR SERVING (OPTIONAL)

Preheat the oven to 350°F. Butter a 10-quart casserole.

In a saucepan, cover the leeks with water and simmer until very tender. Drain, squeeze out the excess moisture, and set aside.

Combine the milk and half-and-half in a large saucepan and scald over medium heat. Gradually stir in the sugar, cornmeal, and flour with a whisk until thick. When the mixture is smooth and creamy, remove from the heat and stir in the butter.

Beat the egg yolks with the heavy cream until light and smooth and add to the cornmeal mixture. Lightly beat in the goat cheese, leeks, and ham.

Whip the egg whites until firm but not dry and fold into the cornmeal mixture. Gently pour into the casserole. Bake for about 20 minutes, until the eggs are set. Serve warm. We like a little warm sorghum on the side.

Chef/Co-Proprietor Tory Miller, L'Etoile (Madison, Wis.)

CŒUR À LA CRÈME

SERVES 8

I had my first cœur à la crème in a funky little restaurant in Berkeley, California, in the early 1970s. It seemed so grown-up and European. This version is made with fresh chèvre, always a good idea. This isn't a last-minute dessert; the cœur à la crème needs to drain for 24 hours.

You'll need cheesecloth and eight individual heart-shaped cœur à la crème molds.

Cœur à la Crème

> 1 POUND FANTÔME FARM FRESH CHÈVRE, AT ROOM TEMPERATURE
>
> ¼ CUP CONFECTIONERS' SUGAR
>
> ½ CUP HEAVY CREAM

Raspberry Sauce

> ¼ CUP SUGAR
>
> 1 PINT FRESH MARKET RASPBERRIES (OR BLUEBERRIES OR STRAWBERRIES)

Garnish

> FRESH RASPBERRIES
>
> FRESH MINT SPRIGS
>
> BISCOTTI OR DECORATIVE COOKIES

To make the cœur à la crème, one day before serving, using a spatula, combine the chèvre with the sugar until smooth. In a separate bowl, whip the cream to soft peaks. Fold into the cheese mixture until thoroughly incorporated.

Line each mold with a square of cheesecloth cut large enough for the ends to cover the mold once it is filled. Fill the mold with the cheese mixture. Cover and refrigerate until the mixture is firmly set, about 24 hours.

To make the raspberry sauce, combine the sugar and 2 tablespoons water in a small saucepan. Cook over medium heat until the sugar caramelizes to a rich amber color.

Add the raspberries and ¼ cup water and allow the mixture to sit for about 10 seconds. Begin stirring the mixture and simmer for about 5 minutes, until the berries are soft.

Remove from the heat and strain through a fine-mesh sieve. Refrigerate the sauce.

When ready to serve, remove the crèmes from the individual molds, place on dessert plates, and discard the cheesecloth. Pour raspberry sauce around each serving. Decorate with fresh raspberries and mint and serve with biscotti.

Triple Walnut Dessert

Adapted from a recipe from Maytag Dairy

SERVES 2

The nice folks at Maytag Dairy originally conceived of this as a salad. I think that if you replace the lettuces with more pears, you get a perfect plate for the end of a meal. Otherwise, it can be the centerpiece of a delicious lunch.

- 1 RIPE COMICE PEAR, CORED AND THINLY SLICED
- 1 RIPE BARTLETT PEAR, CORED AND THINLY SLICED
- ¼ CUP CRUMBLED MAYTAG BLUE CHEESE
- ¼ CUP COARSELY CHOPPED WALNUTS, TOASTED

Sauce

- 6 TABLESPOONS WALNUT OIL
- ¼ CUP PEAR LIQUEUR
- 1 TABLESPOON WALNUT DIJON MUSTARD (REGULAR DIJON IS FINE, TOO)
- FRESHLY GROUND BLACK PEPPER

Arrange the pear slices on two plates. Sprinkle with the cheese and walnuts.

In a small bowl, whisk together the oil, liqueur, mustard, and pepper to taste. Spoon the sauce equally over each plate.

OTHERS TO LOOK FOR

Wisconsin devotes a lot of time, energy, enthusiasm, and milk to cheesemaking and cheese selling. There is huge peer pressure to go with the traditional twentieth-century industrial flow, but there's been a growing understanding of the need for range, for all sorts of every level of style and quality. Additions come slowly on the artisan front, but they're often quite solid and lately very good.

The four brothers of **Crave Brothers Farmstead Cheese** grew up on a forty-acre dairy farm just outside of Beloit, Wisconsin. They started working together on a rented farm in 1978 and purchased their own dairy in 1980. Their farmstead cheese classics include mascarpone, mozzarella, Farmer's Rope String Cheese, and Les Frères.

It's impossible (or just wrong) to write about American cheeses without mentioning **Maytag Dairy Farms'** Maytag Blue. It was one of the first successes of the modern specialty cheese movement. I find it has a Danish blue style of citric zip that's pleasant and uplifting, especially when used in recipes. This cheese has been produced by that famous Maytag washer/dryer family. Others in the clan have chosen their own favorite artisanal efforts—Fritz makes Anchor Steam Beer in the San Francisco Bay Area. Talk about a family focused on pleasing the community.

Another new find from the Gallo Family Vineyards Gold Medal Awards for artisan food folks is the 2008 Dairy Category winner from right in the city of Cleveland, Ohio. **Lake Erie**

Creamery's Blomma is a spray-mold, bloomy-rind goat cheese that has been produced professionally for about two years and is as good as any made for generations in Europe. They also make a nice feta and lovely fromage blanc.

Crave Brothers Farmstead Cheese
W11555 Torpy Road
Waterloo, WI 53594
Tel.: 920-478-4887
Fax: 920-478-4888
www.cravecheese.com

Maytag Dairy Farms
2282 East 8th Street North
Newton, IA 50208
Tel.: 800-247-2458
Fax: 641-792-1567
www.maytagdairyfarms.com

Lake Erie Creamery
3167 Fulton Road, Suite 109
Cleveland, OH 44109
Tel.: 216-961-9222
www.lakeeriecreamery.com

The Wild West

MY GRANDMOTHER'S KITCHEN moved around a lot. For a while it was in a 1930s ranch house in La Crescenta, California, backed by vineyards. Later it was in a three-story pink stucco in the Hollywood Hills. Toward the end, my grandparents smashed a lot of elaborate furniture, some covered in clear plastic, into a frighteningly large 6,000-square-foot mobile home.

Through it all, a few things remained constant. Grandma always had some sort of compote—a stew of fruit and nuts simmered in sugar and juice—in the fridge or on the stove. Melons and tomatoes were always on the windowsill, never chilled, and there was always some sort of fresh cheese, often large simple curds, in a pink or yellow Melmac bowl on the breakfast and the luncheon table. My grandfather, on the other hand, was the keeper of the fruit trees, tomato plants, and occasionally giving vines.

The rest of the West had a pioneering spirit less focused on renovation and resale, on homey farming and overstuffed furniture, than my grandies brought with them from Eastern Europe. In fact,

Father Junipero Serra had some very clear ideas about what he was hoping to establish with his trail of missions, rows of grapevines, and wheels of honest cheese.

Now the country's largest dairy state, and the sixth-largest economy in the world, California has a cheese industry that is even beyond where its wine was in the early '90s: well-established and poised for a boom.

Surprisingly, while the "happy cows" we see on TV abound, it's most likely sheep that should get credit for the West's earliest cheesemaking. It was from the sale of wool and lamb goods that Queen Isabella of Spain got the scratch to finance Columbus, and that later fueled Cortez and other explorers to Cuba, Mexico, and up to California. And there is ample record that our woolly friends were useful passengers as a walking food supply on many of those first trips.

Today, the Petaluma/Tomales Bay region has become a bastion of goat, sheep, and cow's milk cheesemaking that has begun to draw the dedicated and the gifted from all over the world.

I used to joke that there were probably water buffalo out there somewhere in the California underbrush just ready to give us the chance to make real buffalo's milk mozzarella, and now there are! Right outside of L.A., with plans to move up to the northern Sierra foothills sometime soon.

From San Diego Gouda, the Hispanic cheeses of L.A., on up the coast with American originals like Jack and teleme, and up to Washington through Oregon, where blue cheese is made with raw, unhomogenized milk, and washed-rind cheeses may be making a comeback, it certainly is the Wild, Wild West.

CHEESEMAKER:

Sally Jackson
Sally Jackson Cheeses

The best way to truly capture the entirely down-to-earth, straightforward, and plainspoken ways of the Okanogan Highlands of eastern Washington State is to recite a list of Sally Jackson's very fine cheeses. They are: Sally Jackson goat, sheep, and cow. That's it. No fluff or flourishes.

This is a new country to settlers. White people have been in the area since only about 1900. Rough, beautiful, up at 4,200 feet above sea level, with smatterings of views and a few chestnut trees, this 140-acre farm is a real and peaceful haven of focused natural cheesemaking.

The milk comes from well-cared-for animals in thoughtfully managed meadows. When we visited a few years ago, Sally had twenty goats she milked year-round, forty sheep that gave "as they will," and a couple of cows. She showed us short stacks of beautifully handmade cheese molds, of mottled gray and blue ceramic, that reminded us of the steely northern skies.

These days the reputation of Sally Jackson cheese is so solid that nearly every wheel is made to order and sold before it's formed. They are either mold-ripened leaf-wrapped or, for the occasionally larger wheel, pressed into something semi-soft and slightly sweet.

Sally Jackson Cheeses
16 Nealy Road
Oroville, WA 98844
Tel.: 509-485-3722
www.sallyjacksoncheeses.com
jaxon@televar.com

CHEESES:

Goat

Cow

Sheep

Donna and Jim Pacheco
Achadinha Cheese Company

I've been an official judge for the American Cheese Society only twice. The first time was years ago; I think there were about 160 individual entries. In 2002 I believe there were over 1,000 entries.

One judge on each team was a technical expert, usually a professor of dairy something or other. The judges would begin with a 100-point scale and remove points for what they considered flaws.

I was the other sort of judge. We were called aesthetic judges: food professionals such as chefs, shopkeepers, and writers, who fairly dared any food to prove itself to us. But often what the technical judges called flaws we leaped on as delightful and unique character. It was quite a tussle to come up with an evaluation we all agreed on.

I must have been a hit as a judge because just eighteen short years later they asked me back. This time the teams of judges got a category or two to review, from the 400-plus entered. One group was ripened or aged goat cheese and we had a musky old time.

A while after turning in our judging sheets, we got a firm but friendly reprimand. We must not allow three cheeses to end up with the same total, even if they seemed equal. So we went back for retasting, lowered one score, left one alone, and then agreed that the last one really was quite nice and should get one extra point.

That aged, golden, almost caramely goat tomme was called Capricious. Later the same day it won Best of the Entire Show.

Originally made in Eureka, California, these days cheesemaker Donna Pacheco is making her cheese at her own new dairy in the town of Petaluma.

Achadinha Cheese Company and Pacheco Family Dairy

750 Chileno Valley Road

Petaluma, CA 94952

Tel.: 707-763-1025

www.achadinha.com

pachecogoats@aol.com

CHEESES:

Capricious

Broncha

Feta

The Wild West

CHEESEMAKER:

Cindy Callahan
Bellwether Farms

American Cheeses

The hills around Petaluma turn to green from their late-summer tan just days after the first fall or early winter rains. It seems like they should be dotted with plump, fluffy sheep and sweet, heavy cows.

Those pastoral images were more than imagined by Cindy Callahan and son Liam. She finished her earlier careers in law and nursing and was ready for a farm. First it was raising lamb, for keeping their meadows trimmed, then for meat and wool. Soon after, Liam's interest in cheesemaking took him to Italy, and a small herd of Jersey cows next door helped finish their business plan.

Today Bellwether Farms lamb is sold to top restaurants throughout the region. Their sheep cheeses, particularly the delicious Italian-style Pepato, win awards. Their cow's milk selections, now made from another small Jersey herd from the spread on the other side of their land, includes a dreamy

Crescenza, stellar crème fraîche, and a lovely table cheese called Carmody, named for the road at the bottom of their hill. The best is an aged raw milk version, often in short supply, but usually available at one of the better cheese shops around tony Healdsburg.

Bellwether Farms
PO Box 299
Valley Ford, CA 94972
Tel.: 888-527-8606
Fax: 707-795-0300
www.bellwethercheese.com
info@bellwetherfarms.com

CHEESES:

Fromage Blanc

Ricotta

Crème Fraîche

Carmody

Carmody Reserve

Crescenza

San Andreas

Pepato

Sadie Kendall
Kendall Farms

"I want to talk about crème fraîche." It's the message delivered in a booming voice across the phone wires I get every three to ten years from Sadie Kendall, queen of crème fraîche since 1978.

This magical, zippy, thickened cream was, in the 1970s, one of those elemental ingredients that seemed necessary for American cooking to make the leap up onto the world stage. It is made from natural cultured cream and is that rare treasure that is good and satisfying when licked from fingertips, poured over fresh berries, or folded into a favorite recipe.

Sadie has provided a benchmark of dairy goodness that is part of the foundation of this generation's very best foods.

Kendall Farms
PO Box 686
Atascadero, CA 93423
Tel.: 805-466-7252
www.kendallfarmscremefraiche.com
info@kendallfarmscremefraiche.com

PRODUCT:

Crème Fraîche

CHEESEMAKER:
Franklin Peluso
Cal Poly Creamery

Long located in northern California, the main plant of Frank and Franklin Peluso's company moved to Los Banos in the central part of the state once Bay Area real estate got too expensive and the uncertainties of foggy mornings got too unpredictable for teleme cheesemaking.

For quite a while, their collection of Mexican-style cheeses— Cotija, panela, Oxaca, and lovely, creamy *crema*—paid the bills, and teleme, the unctuous, yeasty, rice flour–rubbed six-pound square,

was a labor of love. Then artisan cheesemaking came back into vogue.

Late in 2005, the Pelusos sold the Los Banos company, and Franklin packed up and moved to coastal Maine. There he discovered that teleme, a once all-Holstein-milk cheese, could be done wonderfully with a mixture of Jersey, Guernsey, and Holstein milk. We tried a sample cheese over a Thanksgiving holiday while visiting friends on a 200-acre farm in northern Vermont. Over the long weekend we nearly ate the whole thing.

But cold winters got to be too much for the rest of Franklin's family, so the clan is back in California, now San Luis Obispo, making Franklin's Teleme at Cal-Poly (California Polytechnic State University) right there in the dairy plant, using his same time-honored family recipe.

Franklin Peluso
Cal Poly Creamery
Dairy Science Department
California Polytechnic State University
San Luis Obispo, CA 93407
Franklinsteleme@gmail.com

CHEESES:

Franklin's Teleme
Franklin's Teleme with Peppercorns

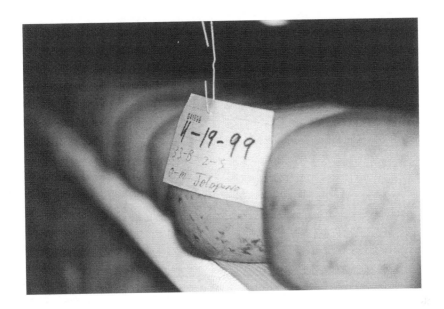

CHEESEMAKER:

Jules Wesselink
Winchester Cheese Company

I hadn't been in the middle of the desert east and south of L.A. since I'd visited my grandparents in the early 1990s in Cathedral City, where Bob Hope had a huge spaceship of a house hanging off the side of a rocky hill. So I guess it was not a total surprise to see a cheese plant entirely made up of adjoining refrigerator trucks (18-wheelers) lined up side by side on a cement slab.

That modular prefab cheese plant was the result of rigorous and costly local production requirements these ready-made units easily satisfied. And Jules Wesselink is on the frugal side. You should see the sort of Rube Goldberg contraptions he's rigged to replicate equipment he could not easily find or afford.

Jules is a jolly, jokey fellow who just got tired of taking care of 400 milking cows and fighting for every dime. Fairly late in life he decided to get into the more traditional family business and make cheese like the Gouda he grew up with. The lessons took, because within a few years of starting out, he flew his cheese back to Holland for the sort of government judging the Dutch embrace, and his scored higher points than any Old World cheese his family had been making for years.

And the cheeses are magnificent. Taste these and you know why one cheese, at various ages and sometimes with assorted spices, can be a real treat.

The Gouda is no longer officially farmstead: he sold the cows. But they're still cared for right next door.

Winchester Cheese Company
32605 Holland Road
Winchester, CA 92596
Tel.: 951-926-4239
Fax: 951-926-3349
www.winchestercheese.com
sales@winchestercheese.com

CHEESES:

Mild Gouda

Medium Aged Gouda

Sharp Gouda

Super Aged Gouda

Jalapeño Gouda

Cumin Gouda

Garden Herb Gouda

Smoked Gouda

Ig Vella
Vella Cheese Company

When it comes to cheesemaking, Ig Vella is nothing short of a national treasure. The man can't help making world-class cheeses.

His family's award-winning dry Jack was created, like many other classics, through need and serendipity. During World War I, when most importing stopped, the Italian communities of northern California had to do without their beloved Parmesan. A wily distributor who discovered some dried Jack cheese forgotten in the corner of a warehouse turned the unsellable into a stand-in. By the next world war, the recipe and presentation had been perfected, and the golden, grateable wheel, now protectively rubbed with a mixture of black pepper, cocoa, and vegetable oil, had found its own place as an American original.

Since those days, Ig has marshaled a host of other world-class tommes to market. His raw milk cheddar is a winning sleeper. His Asiago is a major accomplishment. His mezzo secco, a once nearly forgotten seasonal hybrid cross between what used to be called "fresh" Jack and the dry version, designed to better survive San Francisco's scorching Indian summers, is its own delight.

All of Ig's cheeses seem to have an appropriate Italian twist, but the other real constant is his generosity. He was the first major cheesemaker I'd ever met who always wanted to

acknowledge and praise every line worker, every lead cheesemaker, every clerk and truck driver on his team. He even made sure that his father's legacy in the Rogue Valley of Oregon was put into good hands after his father passed away. For me he's been a benchmark. He may come across as a bit gruff, but his passion is real and his talent extraordinary.

Vella Cheese Company
315 Second Street East
East Sonoma, CA 95476
Tel.: 800-848-0505
Fax: 707-938-4307
www.vellacheese.com
vella@vellacheese.com

CHEESES:

Original High Moisture Monterey Jack

Naturally Seasoned Monterey Jack

Partially Skimmed Monterey Jack

Mezzo Secco

Dry Monterey Jack

Special Select Dry Monterey Jack

Golden Bear Dry Monterey Jack

Sharp Raw Milk Cheddar

Daisy Cheddar

Asiago

Toma

Italian-Style Table Cheese

Romanello

CHEESEMAKER:

Laura Chenel
Laura Chenel's California Chèvre

There is no other cheesemaker in America who has had a more profound influence on the artisan food movement and modern cookery than Laura Chenel. Her fresh chèvre is consistently, simply, the country's best and its creation marked a turning point in how we look at food. She made goat cheese an American pantry staple, helped seduce us with once-exotic greens, and wrote a couple of cheese books way ahead of the cultural curve. Alice Waters's Chez Panisse restaurant's iconic mesclun salad with baked goat cheese could not have happened without Laura.

It was the first day of summer in 1999 when we visited Laura at the famed Stornetta Dairy in southern Sonoma County. The sun was warm and the hillside still mostly green. We went inside the open barn to visit her goats—450 of them—whose every name she seemed to know. They certainly knew her.

Growing up in Sonoma County, she'd helped with the family turkey farm but longed to go to France. She simply loved goats and had to have some. And goats need to give milk, and that milk mustn't be wasted.

Recently, Laura sold her groundbreaking cheese company to a small French firm that had been one she looked up to, even before she began making cheese, nearly thirty years ago. The Triballat

family of the Rians Group knows a lot about supporting small cheesemaking. They've done it for more than half a century and have a portfolio that includes the legendary Époisses and some fine goat's milk cheeses among them.

Laura still spends much of her time next door to the plant, right there on the Stornetta Farm, tending her goats and supplying much of the milk that makes Laura Chenel's California Chèvre an American classic.

American Cheeses

Stornetta Dairy
4310 Fremont Drive
Sonoma, CA 95476
Tel.: 707-996-4477

CHEESES:

Fresh Chèvre	*Peppercorn Chabis*
Plain Chabis	*Cabecou*
Herb Chabis	*Cabecou in Oil*
Dill Chabis	*Tomme*

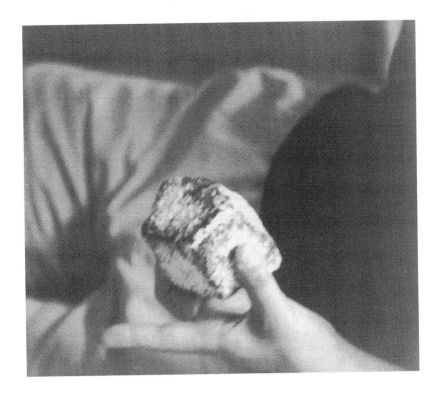

CHEESEMAKER:

Soyoung Scanlan
Andante Dairy

We found the little flat-topped pyramid in the open cheese case of The Food for Thought grocery in Sebastopol. The label said Andante Dairy, Petaluma, in tiny type. The bloomy-mold cheese was earthy and creamy and transporting. I had to know who made this cheese.

As it turned out, Soyoung Scanlan, perhaps America's only fine cheesemaker of Korean decent, was making her delicate cheeses in the very same little plant where Laura Chenel had first started out. This gentle former molecular biologist and part-time assistant to our generation's master of food chemistry, Harold McGee, has been making a collection of diminutive sheep, cow, and goat's milk cheeses for some time. Most have musical names: Metronome, Nocturne; my favorite name is for an unexpected gift of milk she quite rightly turned into something special: Impromptu.

Soyoung is an artist, deeply dedicated to her work, serious about the chemistry but passionate about the art. For the last couple of years, all of her cheeses have been sold before they're made, then delivered at just the right degree of ripening so as to meet the needs of the cheese master (usually it's a fine restaurant chef) who has ordered them.

When we heard from her recently, she was settling into being a new mother, and into her new facility in western Marin County, overlooking Nan McEvoy's luscious, sprawling olive ranch outside of Petaluma.

It was Soyoung who reminded those of us gathered for a small workshop on regional and seasonal cheesemaking a few years ago that natural cycles are all important. "After all," she said, "the animals are making milk for their young, not for us."

I brought some of her cheeses with me to a recent Christmas celebration with friends in Little Washington, Virginia. After a spectacular Christmas Eve feast at the famed Inn at Little Washington and an amazing spread Christmas Day, I was touched when the cheese tray brought an awed pause to the quite sophisticated group around the holiday table.

Andante Dairy

Tel.: 707-769-1379

www.andantedairy.com

soyoungk@andantedairy.com

CHEESES:

COW'S MILK

Nocturne

Pianoforte

Cadenza

Legato

Impromptu (can be cow, goat, or mixed)

GOAT'S MILK

Adagio

Acapella

Figaro

Pastoral Fresh Goat

Crottin

TRIPLE CRÈME

Minuet

Picolo

Largo

MIXED MILK

Melange

Rondo

Metronome

The Wild West

Bingham Hill

I know that Bingham Hill has been well known in better cheese
circles for their Rustic Blue. It was among the first western veiny
cheeses I found to be consistently delicious and, while reminiscent
of other cheeses like Stilton and Blue Cheshire, completely
unique and world-class in its own right. But I must admit, it
was their Poudre Puffs and Tumbleweeds I came to crave. These
gently pasteurized (yes, there are degrees, and finesse counts)
nonhomogenized cow's milk, hand-ladled and formed, spray-mold
fluffy balls have given me great pleasure and feel like the best kind
of indulgence.

We'd brought them home anytime we could from our
wonderful new local wine and cheese merchants, Sophie's Cellars,
in the neighboring town of Monte Rio, by our cabin in the woods
at Sonoma's Russian River.

In 2006, some of the Bingham success brought ultimate
failure. Ramping up for a big client seemed like a dream come
true until the retailer decided to switch gears and focus on other
cheeses. The result was a business collapse and ultimately a
liquidation auction. Thus is the fragility of even celebrated and
successful cheesemakers. There's hope for a return to cheesemaking, as they won their suit to keep hold of the trademarked
names and methods. We can only wait and see.

CHEESEMAKER:

Peggy Smith and Sue Conley
Cowgirl Creamery

One of the original goals dear to the hearts of the women who
started Tomales Bay Foods in the little town of Point Reyes
Station, California, was to help establish a "regional identity
for cheese producers along the coast." They must have been
particularly pleased some years later when the late R. W. "Johnny"
Apple in *The New York Times* referred to their region as "a new
Normandy north of the Bay."

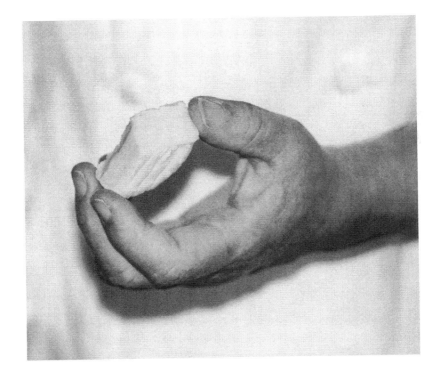

At first simply major boosters of regional and international fine foods, Sue Conley and Peggy Smith have become major award-winning cheesemakers and highly successful, beloved merchants as well. Their handmade organic cheeses, offered under the Cowgirl Creamery label, are mostly made right there, behind a glass wall, off the entrance to their barnlike store or at their pristine new creamery in Petaluma.

One that stands out in great demand at their shops (along with the others in the wildly popular Ferry Building Marketplace in San Francisco and in their hometown of Washington, D.C.) is a classic "mistake" cheese. Spray-mold ripening was interrupted by errant and random stuff growing on an experimental cheese, so they washed it with a little brine (salt water) and produced a delicious washed-rind winner called Red Hawk.

Their devotion to the milk, the making, and the careful ripening of anyone's good cheese has helped them and many others grow. They also thoughtfully handle (ripen and sell) wonderful cheeses made by others.

Cowgirl Creamery Mail Order Corral
Online and Mail Order
Tel.: 866-433-7834
www.cowgirlcreamery.com
mailorder@cowgirlcreamery.com

Cowgirl Creamery Cheese Shop at the Ferry Plaza
1 Ferry Building, #17
San Francisco, CA 94111
Tel.: 415-362-9354
Fax: 415-362-9355

Cowgirl Creamery at Tomales Bay Foods
80 Fourth Street
Point Reyes Station, CA 94956
Tel.: 415-663-9335
Fax: 415-663-5418

Cowgirl Creamery in Washington, D.C.
919 F Street NW
Penn Quarter
Washington, DC 20004
Tel.: 202-393-6880
Fax: 202-393-6883

CHEESES:

Mt. Tam   Cottage Cheese
Red Hawk   Fromage Blanc
St. Pat   Crème Fraîche
Pierce Pt.

The Wild West

Jennifer Lynn Bice
Redwood Hill Farm and Creamery

The original Redwood Hill Dairy sat in one of the prettiest spots I've ever seen. Down a country road and perched on a hill overlooking the gorgeous Iron Horse Vineyards, it was a picturesque fantasy setting in western Sonoma County. There were sweeping orchard views, and, in late winter, blankets of bright yellow mustard flowers blooming under the dormant grapevines.

The farm was built in the late 1960s and taken over by Jennifer Lynn Bice and the late Steven Schack. First and most

commonly known in the area for a very pleasing goat yogurt, Redwood Hill got so productive that Jennifer had to move the cheesemaking to larger quarters. The company now inhabits an old apple warehouse right on Highway 116, called the Gravenstein Highway after the early-harvest heirloom apples that still grow on either side, where she produces a host of accessible, lovely cheeses.

Their award-winning, signature cheese is a delicious bloomy-rind round created in 1997 and called Camellia. It is a favorite of local chefs, who work carefully to bring it along to molten ripeness.

The farm and cheese plant have long employed an ever-rotating parade of mostly Eastern European interns, keeping the business lively and international. Now led by the very talented Peter Kindel, formerly of Haystack Mountain Goat Dairy in Colorado, the cheeses are better than ever.

Redwood Hill Farm and Creamery

2064 Highway 116 North

Building 1, Suite 130

Sebastopol, CA 95472

Tel.: 707-823-8250

Fax: 707-823-6976

www.redwoodhill.com

contact@redwoodhill.com

CHEESES:

Chèvre (traditional and flavored)

Feta

Camellia

California Crottin

Bucheret

Goat Milk Yogurt

Joe Matos
Joe Matos Cheese Factory

This is the sort of cheese that will most likely never appear on the tasting board of every four-star restaurant across America. Not that it isn't as good as any cheese out there. It's just that the Matos family of Santa Rosa doesn't make a big deal about their cheese. They just make world-class wheels.

I offer the Azores-style St. George as an example of how one cheese, with perfectly balanced flavors, consistently pleasing texture, and real complexity and depth, can be a completely satisfying stand-alone food, or an ingredient in a dish with just two or three elements. It's that good.

This is a semi-soft, rubbed (and dry) rind table cheese that sounds and seems a whole lot simpler than it turns out to be. It comes and goes in the markets and cheese counters around the area, but it's always worth the wait.

Joe Matos Cheese Factory
3669 Llano Road
Santa Rosa, CA 95407
Tel.: 707-584-5283

CHEESE:

St. George

Mary Keehn
Cypress Grove Chèvre

Mary Keehn seems like the kind of person you'd really love to have as your mother, or your sister, or a really good friend. There's an earth-mother warmth and a calming wave that comes from this vibrant, talented person whenever she walks into a room.

Cypress Grove Humboldt Fog is one of the great grown-up cheese successes of America's current—and by that I mean in the last few decades—crop of specialty choices. It's a stellar mold-ripened cheese, with a dusting of ash on the outside and in a thin line across the center. Mary says that when they cut the wheel it's reminiscent of the early morning fog way up there in the redwood trees of Mendocino County. It comes in a couple of sizes; the four-pound wheel, a one-pound round and a new eight-ounce Fog Lights version without the center line. They're all delicious.

Cypress Grove Chèvre
1330 Q Street
Arcata, CA 95521
Tel.: 707-825-1100
Fax: 707-825-1101
www.cypressgrovechevre.com
info@cypressgrovechevre.com

CHEESES:

Bermuda Triangle

Goat Milk Cheddar

Fresh Chèvre

Purple Haze

Midnight Moon

Lamb Chopper

Fromage Blanc

Humboldt Fog

Fog Lights

Mad River Roll

Truffle Tremor

CHEESEMAKER:

Cary Bryant and David Gremmels
Rogue Creamery

When we visited the Rogue Creamery in the Rogue River Valley of southern Oregon, we'd just come down from Washington State, so it felt like outer, outer northern California. We were well past the "Last Espresso for 100 Miles" signs up further north and ready to see some familiar country.

The creamery was in transition. Tom Vella, who'd bought the plant from the co-op folks who founded it in 1928, took over in 1935, and started making superior blue-veined cheeses, had passed away, and his son Ig, of Vella Cheese Company, in Sonoma, California, was making the regular commute to keep things going.

Rejecting any number of more than lucrative offers, Ig settled on Cary Bryant and David Gremmels to carry on the tradition of hand-milled cheeses. Soon after, the new boys snagged a London Best at the World Cheese Awards for the famous blue, for which they still use the original cultures. Not a bad start.

So far they're usually up to five very distinct blue cheeses: four cow's milk and one with a blend of cow and goat's milk, one cold-smoked over hazelnut shells. They've established a four-year apprenticeship program, with Ig teaching the sensory evaluation (otherwise known as taste training) part of the first year. And they continue to be an integral part of the local community and the growing world of American cheesemaking.

The Rogue Creamery

311 North Front Street

Central Point, OR 97502

Tel.: 541-664-1537; 866-396-4704

Fax: 541-665-1133

www.roguecreamery.com

info@roguecreamery.com

CHEESES:

Crater Lake Blue

Echo Mountain Blue

Oregon Blue

Oregonzola

Smokey Blue

Rogue River Blue

Lora Lea and Rick Misterly
Quillisascut Cheese Company

Some of the most delicious wine I've ever tasted, made in the style of a musky, sexy red Burgundy, came from the basement of a farmhouse at 1,700 feet above sea level in Rice, Washington.

Our hosts, the delightful and clearly talented Lora Lea and Rick Misterly, kept apologizing for their simple "homemade plonk" and their current batch of not-yet-perfectly-ripened cheeses. She's the cheesemaker, and whatever she crafts is the ingredient of choice for top chefs, especially in Seattle and Portland. The wheels were young, but you could clearly taste and sense the structure, and I was reminded that early into the life of a well-made cheese, you can begin to taste the greatness.

These are people who love their life. Outside their door was a row of grapevines, each a different variety that only hinted at the range of flavors understood and enjoyed by Lora Lea in her life and in her cheesemaking.

Quillisascut Cheese Company
2409 Pleasant Valley Road
Rice, WA 99167
Tel.: 509-738-2011
www.quillisascutcheese.com
loralea@quillisascutcheese.com

CHEESES:

Curado

Viejo

UFO

CHEESEMAKER:

Marin French Cheese Company

On a lovely spring day we stood outside California's oldest cheese factory in the rolling hills of Marin County; the pond, the picnic tables, the old Rouge et Noir Fancy Cheeses sign by the side of the road.

The cellar is the original from 1865. The cows have been gone since the early 1900s, but the company, now owned by James Boyce, is having a major resurgence. I've always loved their slightly nutty, slightly stinky Schloss, a mild washed-rind yeasty rectangle.

They've gotten accolades for their creamy Petite Crème, their soft-ripened blue, and their Triple Crème Brie, which won a gold medal at the World Cheese Awards in London in early 2005. It was a first for an American pasteurized bloomy-rind entry, and a pleasant validation that American cheeses can indeed compete internationally.

This is one of those cheese places that anyone can visit, that busloads of schoolkids can troop through to learn a little something about the last century and a half of local dairy works and also get a nibble of some timeless, world-class cheeses. Pick and choose which you prefer, but stop by for a wander and some lunch.

Marin French Cheese Company

7500 Red Hill Road

Petaluma, CA 94952

Tel.: 800-292-6001

Fax: 707-762-0430

www.marinfrenchcheese.com

cheesefactory@marinfrenchcheese.com

CHEESES:

Camembert

Brie

Triple Crème Brie

Pesto Brie

Peppercorn Brie

Tomato-Basil Brie

Jalapeño Brie

Garlic Brie

Breakfast Cheese

Schloss

Wine Cheese

American Cheeses

Chef Thierry Rautureau, Rover's (Seattle)
QUILLISASCUT GOAT CHEESE IN PHYLLO WITH RATATOUILLE

SERVES 4

Our drive through Washington State was long and . . . well, long. I have vivid memories of coffee kiosks in the middle of what seemed to be nowhere.

This recipe was tested by my old friend Mauney Kaseberg, who has been working on the Rover's cookbook with the restaurant's very talented chef, Thierry Rautureau.

Ratatouille

- 6 TEASPOONS PURE OLIVE OIL
- ½ RED ONION, FINELY DICED
- ¾ TEASPOON MINCED GARLIC
- ¾ TEASPOON MINCED FRESH THYME
- 1 RED BELL PEPPER, CORED, SEEDED, PEELED, AND FINELY DICED
- 1 YELLOW BELL PEPPER, CORED, SEEDED, PEELED, AND FINELY DICED
- 3 TEASPOONS EXTRA VIRGIN OLIVE OIL
- 1 TEASPOON MINCED FRESH CHIVES
- SALT AND FRESHLY GROUND WHITE PEPPER
- 1 SHALLOT, MINCED
- 1 SMALL ZUCCHINI, SEEDED AND FINELY DICED
- ½ SMALL EGGPLANT, PEELED, SEEDED, AND FINELY DICED
- 6 FRESH BASIL LEAVES, FINELY SLICED

Sancerre Sauce

   1 CUP SANCERRE OR OTHER SAUVIGNON BLANC

   2 SHALLOTS, THINLY SLICED

   1/2 TEASPOON MINCED GARLIC

   3/4 CUP VEGETABLE STOCK

   1/2 CUP HEAVY CREAM

   5 OUNCES GOAT CHEESE CAILLÉ (JUST SET) OR
      OTHER FRESH GOAT CHEESE (ABOUT 1/2 CUP)

   1/4 TEASPOON MINCED FRESH THYME

   SALT

Phyllo-Cheese Packets

   1 LARGE EGG YOLK

   SALT

   3 SHEETS PHYLLO DOUGH

   4 TABLESPOONS (1/2 STICK) UNSALTED BUTTER,
      MELTED, PLUS EXTRA IF NEEDED

   4 SMALL GOAT CHEESE CROTTINS

   2 TABLESPOONS UNSALTED BUTTER

   3/4 CUP SKINNED FAVA BEANS

   PINCH OF MINCED GARLIC

   PINCH OF MINCED FRESH THYME

   FRESHLY GROUND WHITE PEPPER

Garnish

   BASIL OIL

   4 FRESH BASIL LEAVES

   RED BELL PEPPER COULIS

   YELLOW BELL PEPPER COULIS

To make the ratatouille, line a rimmed baking sheet with paper towels.

Heat 2 teaspoons of the pure olive oil in a large skillet over medium heat. Add the onion, ¼ teaspoon of the garlic, and ¼ teaspoon of the thyme. Sauté until aromatic, about 1 minute, then add the red and yellow bell peppers, increase the heat to medium-high, and sauté until tender, stirring often, 1 to 2 minutes longer. Stir in 1 teaspoon of the extra virgin olive oil and ½ teaspoon of the chives. Season lightly with salt and pepper and transfer to the baking sheet, spreading the peppers out so they cool; set aside.

Heat another 2 teaspoons of the pure olive oil in the skillet over medium-high heat. Add the shallot, another ¼ teaspoon of the garlic, and another ¼ teaspoon of the thyme. Sauté until aromatic, about 1 minute, then add the zucchini and sauté until tender, stirring often, 1 to 2 minutes longer. Stir in 1 teaspoon of the extra virgin olive oil, season lightly with salt and pepper, and add the zucchini to the peppers, spreading it out evenly to cool.

Heat the remaining 2 teaspoons pure olive oil in the skillet over medium-high heat. Add the eggplant with the remaining ¼ teaspoon garlic and ¼ teaspoon thyme. Sauté, stirring often, until tender, 2 to 3 minutes. Stir in the remaining 1 teaspoon extra virgin olive oil and the remaining ½ teaspoon chives, and season lightly with salt and pepper. Add to the baking sheet, spreading the eggplant out evenly. Scatter the basil over and stir gently to mix the vegetables.

To make the sauce, combine the wine, shallots, and garlic in a medium saucepan and bring to a boil over medium-high heat. Simmer until reduced by about half, 5 to 7 minutes. Add the vegetable stock and reduce again by about half, 4 to 5 minutes. Add the cream and reduce by about one-third, 8 to 10 minutes. Transfer the mixture to a blender and add the goat cheese and thyme. Blend until smooth, then strain the sauce through a fine sieve into a small saucepan. Taste the sauce for seasoning, adding salt to taste. Keep warm over very low heat.

To make the cheese packets, preheat the oven to 375°F. Line a baking sheet with parchment paper.

Blend the egg yolk in a small bowl with 1 teaspoon of water and a pinch of salt until smooth. Set aside.

Set 1 phyllo sheet on the counter. (Keep the rest covered to prevent drying out.) Brush the top of the sheet lightly but thoroughly with melted butter. Lay another phyllo sheet on top, lining up the edges as evenly as possible. Butter this sheet, top with the third sheet, and butter it as well. Cut into quarters.

Spoon 2 tablespoons of the ratatouille into the center of each piece of phyllo and top with a goat cheese crottin. Fold the phyllo edges up over the cheese to fully enclose it, pleating the edges neatly and securely. Turn the packet over, brush the top with the egg yolk glaze, and set on the parchment-lined baking sheet. Bake until the phyllo is crisp and nicely browned, about 15 minutes. Set aside the remaining ratatouille.

While the packets are baking, melt the 2 tablespoons butter in a small skillet over medium heat. Add the fava beans and cook, stirring often, until tender but not browned, 5 to 7 minutes. Add the garlic and thyme with salt and pepper to taste. Toss gently to mix and keep warm over low heat. Reheat the remaining ratatouille in a small skillet over medium-low heat.

To serve, spoon a flat circle of the ratatouille to one side of each plate and top with a phyllo packet. Spoon the Sancerre sauce around and spoon the fava beans into a small pile alongside the phyllo. Drizzle the top of the phyllo and perimeter of the plate with some basil oil and tuck a basil leaf alongside the phyllo packet. Add dots of red and yellow bell pepper coulis around the plate and serve right away.

Laura Chenel

BAKED GOAT CHEESE SALAD

This is the recipe that led the American cheese revolution. It taught us that each leaf could have its own world of flavors, and that the best leaves changed with the season. It gently introduced mild yet distinct and consistently delicious goat cheese and helped kick off a boom of what many called California cuisine. The fad for putting goat cheese on every salad has receded, but the pervasive influence on the American table is undeniable. We try to have it at least four times a year at the Café at Chez Panisse.

8 OUNCES LAURA CHENEL FRESH GOAT CHEESE

1¼ CUPS EXTRA VIRGIN OLIVE OIL

3 TO 4 SPRIGS FRESH THYME, CHOPPED

1 SPRIG FRESH ROSEMARY, CHOPPED

½ SOURDOUGH BAGUETTE

1 TABLESPOON RED WINE VINEGAR

1 TEASPOON SHERRY VINEGAR

SALT AND FRESHLY GROUND BLACK PEPPER

2 CUPS GARDEN LETTUCE LEAVES

Slice the goat cheese into 8 disks, each about ½ inch thick. Pour 1 cup of the olive oil over the disks and sprinkle with the chopped thyme and rosemary. Cover and store in a cool place for several hours or up to a week.

Preheat the oven to 300°F. Cut the baguette in half lengthwise and bake for about 20 minutes, until dry and lightly colored. Grate into fine crumbs on a box grater or in a food processor. (The crumbs can be made in advance and stored.)

Heat the oven to 400°F. Remove the cheese from the marinade and roll in the bread crumbs, coating thoroughly. Place on a baking sheet and bake for 6 minutes, until the cheese is warm.

Combine the vinegars in a small bowl with a pinch of salt. Whisk in the remaining ¼ cup oil and a little pepper. Taste for seasoning and adjust.

Toss the lettuce lightly with the vinaigrette. Divide among four plates. Carefully place 2 disks of cheese over the greens and serve.

Tea and Tarot

SONOMA TOAST

SERVES 1 OR 2

On the stretch of Highway 116, dotted with antique and
"collectibles" shops just outside of Sebastopol, there's a wonderful
old building called the Antique Society, housing hundreds of
stalls. Just by the front door is a small shop previously occupied by
an amazing chocolate maker called La Dolce V. The lemon squares
are a particular favorite, and tea or a perfect organic espresso
comes in any one of a number of lovely teacups and saucers on
hand-painted trays, sometimes with cloth doilies. La Dolce V has
moved on, but their replacement (at this writing) is a lovely bakery
shop called Sfoglia, or, literally, "Little Leaf," named for the Italian
word for puff pastry.

Before La Dolce V inhabited the space, Tea and Tarot was
there. You ordered tea and snacks and the woman read your tarot
cards. No extra charge. Food offerings were minimal, but one
was and still is among my favorite local nibbles. It shows how
complete, complex, and delicious cheese can be.

2 SLICES COUNTRY-STYLE SOURDOUGH BREAD

2 OR 3 SLICES ST. GEORGE CHEESE FROM JOE
MATOS CHEESE FACTORY

1 TOMATO, SLICED

1 TEASPOON BALSAMIC VINEGAR

1 TEASPOON EXTRA VIRGIN OLIVE OIL

2 TEASPOONS CHOPPED FRESH HERBS OF CHOICE

Lightly toast the bread. Top with the cheese and melt under the
broiler. Top with the sliced tomato and drizzle with the balsamic
vinegar and olive oil. Finish with a sprinkle of chopped herbs.

Chefs Mary Sue Milliken and Susan Feniger
Border Grill (Los Angeles)

GREEN CHICKEN CHILAQUILES CASSEROLE

SERVES 6 TO 8

I'd probably try anything cooked by America's Too Hot Tamales, Mary Sue Milliken and Susan Feniger, at Border Grill. Here's something homey and easy that uses three of the many first-rate American-made cheeses of Mexican heritage.

> 2 WHOLE CHICKEN BREASTS, SPLIT
>
> SALT AND FRESHLY GROUND BLACK PEPPER
>
> 2 CUPS CHICKEN STOCK
>
> 3½ CUPS TOMATILLO SALSA (PAGE 235)
>
> ½ CUP HEAVY CREAM
>
> I ONION, SLICED PAPER THIN
>
> ½ CUP VEGETABLE OIL
>
> 12 DAY-OLD CORN TORTILLAS (PREFERABLY HOMEMADE; 18 TO 24 FOR INDIVIDUAL CASSEROLES)
>
> I CUP GRATED MANCHEGO CHEESE
>
> I CUP GRATED PANELA CHEESE
>
> ½ CUP GRATED AÑEJO CHEESE

Season the chicken all over with salt and pepper. Bring the chicken stock to a boil in a large saucepan. Place the chicken in the stock, reduce the heat to medium, cover, and cook until the meat is tender, about 15 minutes. Set aside and let the chicken cool in the stock. While the chicken is cooling, preheat the oven to 350°F.

When the chicken is cool, remove the skin and bones and shred the meat into bite-size pieces. Strain and reserve the stock for another use.

In a large bowl, combine the fresh tomatillo salsa, cream, 1 teaspoon salt, ½ teaspoon pepper, onion, and chicken.

Heat the oil in a medium skillet over medium-low heat. Cook the tortillas for just about 5 seconds per side to soften, then transfer to a large colander to drain.

Butter a 4-quart casserole or 6 to 8 individual casseroles. Combine the cheeses in a mixing bowl.

Spread a thin layer of the cheese mixture over the bottom of the baking dish. Push the solids in the bowl of chicken and salsa to the side so the liquids form in a pool in the bottom. One by one, dip the softened tortillas in the pool to moisten. Layer one-third of the tortillas over the cheese and top with half of the chicken mixture with its sauce. Sprinkle half of the remaining cheese over the chicken. Repeat the tortilla, chicken, and cheese layers, ending with a layer of tortillas on top.

Cover tightly with aluminum foil and bake for 30 minutes or until the edges are slightly brown. Remove the foil and let sit for 10 minutes before slicing and serving.

TOMATILLO SALSA

MAKES 3½ CUPS

- 1 POUND TOMATILLOS, HUSKED, WASHED, AND QUARTERED
- 2 TO 4 LARGE JALAPEÑOS, STEMMED, SEEDED IF DESIRED, AND ROUGHLY CHOPPED
- ½ MEDIUM ONION, CUT IN HALF
- 2 BUNCHES CILANTRO, LEAVES AND STEMS
- 2 TEASPOONS SALT

Place the tomatillos, jalapeños, and ½ cup water in a blender or food processor fitted with the metal blade. Puree just until chunky. Add the onion, cilantro, and salt and puree for about 2 minutes more, until no large chunks remain. (This salsa keeps in the refrigerator, in a covered container, for about 3 days.)

Chef Greg Ische, Hotel del Coronado (San Diego)

WINCHESTER GOUDA AND BASIL GNOCCHI WITH PORCINI AND ASPARAGUS RAGOUT

SERVES 2 AS A MAIN COURSE, 4 AS AN APPETIZER

First you get a sous-chef or two . . . This delightful recipe from the former executive chef of the famed Hotel del Coronado is a lot of work but not terribly difficult. It's mostly an excuse to gently feature the Winchester aged Gouda from not far away and is a good example of how the sharp, almost caramelized tang of this cheese is so delicious and a complete departure from the expected Parmesan. Greg Ische now acts as manager of culinary services for a development department of Nestlé in Cleveland, Ohio. Talk about having a room full of helpers.

Store-bought potato gnocchi may be used in place of the fresh handmade gnocchi.

Gnocchi

- I POUND RUSSET POTATOES
- KOSHER SALT
- 3 OR 4 LARGE EGGS
- PINCH OF FRESHLY GRATED NUTMEG
- FRESHLY GROUND BLACK PEPPER
- ¼ CUP FINELY GRATED WINCHESTER GOUDA, PREFERABLY SUPER-AGED
- I CUP ALL-PURPOSE FLOUR, PLUS EXTRA FOR DUSTING
- LEAVES FROM ½ BUNCH BASIL, FINELY SHREDDED

Ragout

2 TABLESPOONS UNSALTED BUTTER

¼ SWEET ONION, DICED (ABOUT ¼ CUP)

1 CLOVE GARLIC, CHOPPED

4 OUNCES FRESH PORCINI MUSHROOMS,
  SLICED THICK

1 BUNCH JUMBO ASPARAGUS, TIPS ONLY,
  BLANCHED AND COOLED

3 TOMATOES, PEELED, CORED, SEEDED,
  AND CUT INTO THIN STRIPS

KOSHER SALT AND FRESHLY GROUND BLACK PEPPER

Finishing and garnish

1 TABLESPOON OLIVE OIL

½ CUP DRY WHITE WINE

½ CUP CHICKEN STOCK

2 TABLESPOONS UNSALTED BUTTER

KOSHER SALT AND FRESHLY GROUND BLACK PEPPER

LEAVES FROM ½ BUNCH BASIL, FINELY SHREDDED

SHAVED EXTRA SHARP WINCHESTER GOUDA,
  AS NEEDED

To make the gnocchi, preheat the oven to 425°F. Place the potatoes on a bed of kosher salt and bake until soft, about 1 hour. Cut the potatoes in half and scoop out the flesh. (Discard the skins or set aside for another use.) Pass the potato flesh through a food mill into a bowl. Let cool slightly.

Whisk 3 eggs lightly to blend in a large bowl. Add the potatoes, nutmeg, ½ teaspoon salt, about ¼ teaspoon pepper, and the cheese. Stir gently until blended. Add the flour and knead until the dough is firm but yielding. The dough should be somewhat moist, yet hold a shape, and able to be rolled out on a floured surface without sticking. If necessary, add the fourth egg or knead in more flour. Knead in the basil.

Sprinkle flour over a work surface and a parchment-lined baking sheet. On the floured surface, roll pieces of dough into a rope the thickness of your thumb. Cut into lengths of about 1½ inches. Roll each piece over the back of a fork or between gnocchi paddles to make grooves. Place the gnocchi on the baking sheet in a single layer. Continue until all the dough has been shaped. (The gnocchi may be frozen, well wrapped, for up to 1 month.)

Bring a large pot of salted water to a boil. Add the gnocchi, being careful not to let them stick together. Let them rise to the top of the boiling water, then cook for about 2 minutes. Gently drain in a colander and set aside.

To make the ragout, melt 1 tablespoon of the butter in a large sauté pan over medium-high heat. When it is foaming, add the onion and garlic. Sauté until golden. Add the second tablespoon of butter and the porcini, and sauté until the mushrooms are soft. Add the asparagus and tomatoes, season with salt and pepper, and sauté lightly. Set aside to keep warm.

To finish, heat the olive oil in a large sauté pan over high heat. Add the gnocchi and sauté until browned and lightly crisp. Stir in the wine and cook until almost dry. Add about half of the chicken stock and the butter, and cook until the sauce is thick. If necessary, add more stock to keep it loose. Season with salt and pepper.

To serve, divide the gnocchi among the plates. Top with the ragout. Garnish with the basil and cheese, and serve immediately.

Chef Hubert Keller, Fleur de Lys *(San Francisco)*

CRISP SWEETBREADS ON A FONDUE OF YOUNG LEEKS AND TRIPLE CREAM BRIE

SERVES 4 AS AN APPETIZER

This is a pretty complicated recipe from an enormously appealing chef. It's the sort of fantasy dish I like to read through, slowly, before I call to make a reservation at the really wonderful sort of restaurant Hubert Keller works so hard to maintain. His strengths include truly sumptuous food offered with warmth and not an ounce of pretension. It's a lot of work, and worth leaving to the pros.

- 1½ POUNDS VEAL SWEETBREADS
- 1 SMALL ONION
- 1 BOUQUET GARNI
- SALT AND FRESHLY GROUND BLACK PEPPER
- 1 TABLESPOON CUMIN SEEDS
- 1 TABLESPOON CORIANDER SEEDS
- 2 TEASPOONS HONEY
- 1½ CUPS VEAL DEMI-GLACE (HOMEMADE OR STORE-BOUGHT)
- 16 GREEN ASPARAGUS TIPS, 3 INCHES LONG
- 16 WHITE ASPARAGUS TIPS, 3 INCHES LONG
- 12 CAULIFLOWER FLORETS
- VIRGIN OLIVE OIL
- 1 SMALL LEEK, WHITE AND TENDER GREEN PARTS ONLY, CUT IN HALF LENGTHWISE AND SLICED CROSSWISE
- 4 TEASPOONS YUKON GOLD MASHED POTATO
- 2 TEASPOONS TRIPLE CREAM BRIE (NO RIND)

ALL-PURPOSE FLOUR FOR SPRINKLING

6 SMALL CHERRY TOMATOES, HALVED

4 SMALL SPRIGS FRESH CHERVIL

To prepare the sweetbreads, soak them in cold water for 4 to 6 hours. Drain the sweetbreads, place in a saucepan, and cover with fresh cold water. Add the onion, bouquet garni, salt, and pepper and bring to a boil. Lower the heat and simmer for 8 minutes. Remove the sweetbreads and discard the cooking liquid, onion, and bouquet garni. Let cool, then clean the sweetbreads by peeling off any membranes and fat. Cut them into 8 equal slices. Keep refrigerated.

To prepare the sauce, toast the cumin and coriander seeds in a small sauté pan over medium heat for 3 to 4 minutes. Add the honey and cook for another minute. Add the demi-glace and simmer gently for 3 to 4 minutes. Adjust the seasoning. Strain out the seeds. The sauce is ready; keep warm in a small saucepan.

To prepare the vegetables, bring a saucepan of salted water to a boil and blanch the green and white asparagus for 4 to 5 minutes or until just tender. Immediately transfer to an ice bath. When cool, drain and set aside. Using the same water, blanch the cauliflower florets for 4 to 5 minutes or until tender. Immediately transfer to an ice bath. When cool, drain and set aside.

To prepare the fondue of leek, heat ½ teaspoon olive oil in a heavy-bottomed saucepan. Add the leek, season with salt and pepper, and sweat over medium heat for 8 to 10 minutes until very soft but not colored. Add the mashed potato and the Brie. Stir gently. Check the seasoning and keep hot.

To finish the dish, season the sweetbreads with salt and pepper and coat lightly with flour, shaking off any excess. Heat ½ teaspoon olive oil in a heavy-bottomed sauté pan and sauté the sweetbreads over medium heat, turning occasionally, for 5 to 6 minutes or until browned and crisp. At the same time, heat the cauliflower in another small sauté pan with ¼ teaspoon olive oil; season with salt and pepper. Separately heat up the green and white asparagus in ½ teaspoon olive oil; season with salt and pepper.

To assemble the dish, arrange 4 green asparagus in the center of each warm serving plate, the tips pointing to your left. In between each green asparagus, place a white asparagus, the tip pointing to your right. Top the asparagus with a large spoonful of leek and Brie fondue. Top the fondue with 2 slices of sweetbreads. Spoon the sauce around the asparagus and place 3 cauliflower florets around the plate on the sauce. Top each floret with a cherry tomato half. Top the sweetbreads with a bouquet of chervil. Serve immediately.

The Wild West

Chef Richard Sandoval, Tamayo (Denver)
WILD MUSHROOM, REQUEZON, AND EPAZOTE QUESADILLAS

SERVES 8 AS AN APPETIZER

Mexico City–born Richard Sandoval is quite busy these days bringing his personal take on Latin cooking to a lot of people in some interesting cities. In addition to Tamayo, he has restaurants that include Maya in San Francisco and New York, a seafood spot called Pampano with opera star Placido Domingo, also in New York, Isla Mexican Kitchen & Tequila Bar at Treasure Island in Las Vegas, the multi-culti Zengo (it means "give and take" in Japanese) in Denver and D.C. . . . and then there's that restaurant in Dubai.

His cooking is always special and deeply satisfying. I'd personally try almost any sort of anything called a quesadilla, so this recipe, from chef Josefina Santacrus of Pampano, seems like a perfect choice.

Dough

> 2 CUPS INSTANT CORN MASA MIX FOR TORTILLAS
>
> 1¼ CUPS WARM WATER

Fillings

> 2 TABLESPOONS CANOLA OIL
>
> ⅓ CUP FINELY CHOPPED SPANISH ONION
>
> 1 TO 2 SERRANO CHILES, FINELY CHOPPED (SEEDED IF DESIRED)
>
> 12 OUNCES MIXED WILD MUSHROOMS, CLEANED, STEMMED, AND CHOPPED (SEE NOTE)
>
> ½ TEASPOON SALT
>
> 8 OUNCES REQUEZON CHEESE OR OTHER CREAMY SOFT FRESH CHEESE (ABOUT 1 CUP)
>
> 1 HEAPING TABLESPOON CHOPPED EPAZOTE LEAVES

Salsa Verde

8 OUNCES TOMATILLOS

1½ TEASPOONS CANOLA OIL

¼ CUP CHOPPED SPANISH ONION

1 SERRANO CHILE, ROUGHLY CHOPPED

½ CLOVE GARLIC

1½ TEASPOONS CHOPPED FRESH CILANTRO

SALT

2 QUARTS VEGETABLE OIL

To make the dough, mix together the instant masa and water in a medium bowl. Knead in the bowl until a soft dough forms; if the dough does not hold together, add a little more water. Divide the dough into 16 small balls and cover with a slightly damp kitchen towel.

To make the fillings, heat the oil in a large sauté pan. When hot, add the onion and sauté until translucent. Add the chiles and sauté briefly. Add the mushrooms and sauté until golden, stirring occasionally. Add the salt and set aside to cool. In a separate bowl, combine the Requezon and epazote.

To make the salsa verde, remove the husks from the tomatillos and rinse the tomatillos thoroughly to remove stickiness. Cut into quarters. In a large sauté pan, heat the oil until hot and add the tomatillos and onion. Sauté until lightly browned, about 10 minutes. Add the chile and garlic and sauté for 2 to 3 minutes, until all the vegetables are soft. Transfer to a blender, add the cilantro, and puree. Season with salt and set aside.

To assemble the quesadillas, lay a piece of plastic wrap or waxed paper on the bottom plate of a tortilla press. Place a ball of dough in the center of the press, and lay another piece of plastic on top. Close the press to form a tortilla. Raise the top plate and peel off the plastic.

On one half of the tortilla, place 1 tablespoon of the mushrooms and 1 tablespoon of the cheese mixture. Fold the other half over the filling and press down the sides, making sure the edges are well sealed. You might have to use a little water to help seal the edges. Place on a baking sheet and cover with a damp kitchen towel. Repeat the process, using the rest of the dough and filling.

Heat the vegetable oil to 350°F in a deep pot. Carefully drop in 2 to 4 quesadillas at a time and fry until golden. Remove with a slotted spoon, drain on paper towels, and keep warm. Continue until you have fried all the quesadillas.

Serve 2 quesadillas per person. Drizzle the salsa verde on top or serve on the side.

NOTE: Huitlacoche is a fungus that grows on corn during the rainy season; it is silky black and has a very earthy flavor. It can be found either fresh or canned. You can use it in place of, or combined with, the wild mushrooms.

Chef John Tesar, Rosewood Mansion (Dallas)

CALIFORNIA GOAT CHEESE CHEESECAKE

SERVES 4 TO 6 DEPENDING ON THE SIZE OF THE RAMEKIN

Here's what happens when a chef from New York moves to northern California. He wants to use the local goat cheese and mascarpone, so he makes a cheesecake. Then he dresses it up to serve in a restaurant with a view, Wild Goose, on Lake Tahoe. John Tesar is an intense cook who works hard to make it look easy. He's currently starring as the executive chef at the recently redone and beloved Rosewood Mansion on Turtle Creek in Dallas, but he still likes to snowboard in the Sierras and make goat cheese cheesecake.

- 8 OUNCES LAURA CHENEL FRESH GOAT CHEESE, AT ROOM TEMPERATURE
- 12 OUNCES CREAM CHEESE *OR* 1 1/2 POUNDS MASCARPONE CHEESE, AT ROOM TEMPERATURE
- 1/2 CUP SUGAR, PLUS EXTRA FOR THE RAMEKINS
- 1/2 VANILLA BEAN, SPLIT AND SCRAPED
- 12 OUNCES MASCARPONE CHEESE (IF USING CREAM CHEESE), AT ROOM TEMPERATURE
- 4 LARGE EGGS
- UNSALTED BUTTER, SOFTENED, FOR THE RAMEKINS
- FRESH OR DRIED MISSION FIGS COOKED WITH PORT WINE AND VANILLA, FOR SERVING

In a stand mixer with a paddle, beat the goat cheese, cream cheese (or half of the mascarpone), sugar, and vanilla bean seeds until blended. Add the remaining (or the 12 ounces) mascarpone and beat until smooth. Add the eggs one at a time and mix well. Let the batter rest for 30 minutes.

Meanwhile, preheat the oven to 350°F and bring a kettle of water to a boil. Butter and sugar 3- or 4-inch ramekins or individual soufflé molds. Pour the batter into the ramekins. Place them in a roasting pan several inches deeper than the ramekins. Carefully pour boiling water halfway up the sides of the ramekins. Cover the pan with foil.

Bake for 30 minutes, then remove the pan and release the steam. Re-cover and bake for an additional 15 to 20 minutes, until the cakes have set around the edges.

Remove from the water bath and chill for at least 2 hours or overnight in the refrigerator.

Unmold onto individual plates and serve with the fig compote.

Marion Cunningham's
Empty Plate Mac & Cheese

SERVES 3 OR 4

Over the last nearly forty years, when Marion was not home making waffles for old friends and new acquaintances, or dashing off to dinner at some new or classic San Francisco Bay Area restaurant, or writing another best-selling cookbook, she has loved going to potluck dinners. This recipe is one that always gets raves. We actually named it ourselves from the unstaged, ravaged-plate photo from our tasting. The rest of the meal was a simply dressed Boston lettuce salad, and a dessert of pineapple upside down cake. We recommend additional roughage.

2 TO 3 CUPS ELBOW MACARONI

5 TABLESPOONS MELTED BUTTER

1 CUP SOUR CREAM

2 CUPS GRATED SHARP CHEDDAR CHEESE

1 ¼ CUPS DRY WHITE BREAD CRUMBS

Preheat the oven to 350°F. Bring 2 quarts water to a boil in a large saucepan; add a little salt. Add the macaroni and cook, stirring often, until just tender, about 7 minutes. Don't overcook.

Drain the noodles and transfer them to a baking dish. Add 3 tablespoons of the melted butter, the sour cream, and cheddar. Toss the mixture with a large spoon until the ingredients are well integrated. Taste for salt and add if needed.

Bake for about 15 minutes, until bubbling and lightly browned. Toss the bread crumbs with the remaining 2 tablespoons melted butter. Sprinkle over the top and serve hot.

OTHERS TO LOOK FOR

There are a host of other cheeses being made throughout the Far West. Some are classic in style, but more tend to pop up that reflect the adventurous, sometimes end-of-the-world spirit of the region. I don't much care for fetas with pesto or sun-dried anything, but when innovation meets good taste, I get pretty happy.

I've always loved real fresh cream cheese, which is sometimes referred to as "dried cream." I've gotten good ones in New York, but I really love the taste of the West in this one, which is a real step above. **Sierra Nevada's** all-natural cream cheese (they bought the company I grew up with, called Gina Marie) is, as is all cream cheese, only 20 percent butterfat in solid matter compared to the 80 percent in butter, so go ahead and smear some on a bagel!

Bravo Farms, in the middle of California, gets my vote for top-quality Edam. They also make raw milk cheddars that are popular and what people seem to call "accessible."

Three Sisters Farmstead has won both national and international awards for their handcrafted farmstead cheeses. The Serena is a first-rate aged table cheese, but their newer Serenita shows how they've evolved as talented cheesemakers.

The Giacomini family has been farming in the lush pasture lands of northern California for years. **Point Reyes Original Blue** is the first traditionally made California blue-veined cheese in recent history, but cheesemaking has been in this family for over a hundred years. The wheel is creamy, lightly citric, and very well balanced. It's also beautiful to look at.

There is **Haystack Mountain Goat Dairy** in Colorado, whose Chèvre in Marinade won a first place and Smoked Chèvre that won a second at the American Cheese Society annual competition in 2005. I think we're going to see a lot more good cheese from these folks and from the Rockies.

Then there are the water buffalo currently wintering in controlled pastures near Chico, California, and the mozzarella cheese that is made from their milk in the same traditional style as in Italy in an industrial section of L.A. near Gardena. Yup, it's the real thing, transplanted by a husband-and-wife team who call their company by the original Latin name for the treasured beast, **Bubalus Bubalis.** It's delicious.

The folks at **Beecher's Handmade Cheese** make cheese right in the middle of things at Seattle's famed Pike Place Market. Their flagship cheese is a sort of cheddar-meets-Gruyère experience that is friendly and award winning.

Beecher's Handmade Cheese
1600 Pike Place
Seattle, WA
Tel.: 206-956-1964
www.beechershandmadecheese.com

Sierra Nevada
6505 County Road 39
Willows, CA 95988
Tel.: 530-934-8660
Fax: 530-934-8670
www.sierranevadacheese.com

Bravo Farms
36005 Highway 99
Traver, CA 93673
Tel.: 559-897-4634
Fax: 559-897-4635
www.bravofarms.com

Three Sisters Farmstead Cheese
24163 Road 188
Lindsay, CA 93247
Tel.: 559-562-2132
Fax: 559-562-0911
www.threesisterscheese.com

Point Reyes Original Blue
PO Box 9
Point Reyes Station, CA 94956
Tel.: 800-591-6878
www.pointreyescheese.com

Haystack Mountain Goat Dairy
1121 Colorado Avenue, Suite A
Longmont, CO 80501
Tel.: 720-494-8714
www.haystackgoatcheese.com

Bubalus Bubalis
1207 South Broadway
Gardena, CA 90248
Tel.: 310-515-0500
www.realmozzarella.com

Willamette Valley Cheese
8105 Wallace Road NW
Salem, OR 97304
Tel.: 503-399-9806
www.wvcheeseco.com

Golden Glen Creamery
15098 Field Road
Bow, WA 98232
Tel.: 360-766-MILK
www.goldenglencreamery.com

Pleasant Valley Dairy
6804 Kickerville Road
Ferndale, WA
Tel.: 360-366-5398

Samish Bay Cheese
15115 Bow Hill Road
Bow, WA
Tel.: 360-766-6707
www.samishbaycheese.com

Washington State University
Creamery
PO Box 641122
Pullman, WA 99164
Tel.: 800-457-5442
www.wsu.edu/creamery

The Wild West

Awards, Accolades, and Endorsements

CARAMEL MASCARPONE COULD CERTAINLY BE A delightful dessert when created and prepared by a talented, fanciful chef. But (for me, at least) it can't be a cheese. Likewise the words "award-winning" and "herb, spice, and garlic cheese spread" should most likely never be used in the same sentence.

How exactly can any of us out here judge the quality of newly discovered cheeses when so many awards are given for what often seems to be no more than fairly tasty near-food of questionable methodology and sometimes frightening ingredients?

That's not to say that the above-mentioned specialties are in some way wrong, evil, or even untraditional. But award-winning is another matter.

The American Cheese Society seemed to be the group that would help move lovers of America's aged and ripened cheeses in a new direction. Less obsessed with creating the world's largest wheel or discussing the oddest combinations, the ACS awards have shined a light on some truly noteworthy results of cheesemaking at its best. Gold medals have saved family farms and established national benchmarks. Alas, as with so much that becomes successful in America, there is now constant pressure to push things to a higher profile, a larger audience, and—make no mistake—greater profits, which don't always make for great cheese.

With any luck, they'll soon figure out how best to separate the most successfully made artisan, specialty, and farmstead cheeses from the more industrial and tricked-out ones, but in the meantime, look to awards as a heads-up for great possibilities. Trust some of the palates in your sphere of reading and shopping, look to your local cheesemonger (okay, shop clerk) for advice, accept that taste when offered across the counter, and, most important, trust yourself to find and enjoy what is right for you.

AWARDS

The American Cheese Society
Annual Judging and Competition
www.cheesesociety.org/displaycommon.cfm?an=1&subarticlenbr=74

The American Cheesemakers Awards
www.cheeseawards.com

Wisconsin Cheese Makers Association
Biennial World Championship Cheese Contest
www.wischeesemakersassn.org/wccc/2008/index.html

Gallo Family Vineyards Gold Medal Awards
www.gallosonoma.com/goldmedal/home.htm

Nantwich International Cheese Show

Nantwich Agricultural Society, Limited

www.nantwichshow.co.uk

The World Cheese Awards

The Guild of Fine Foods, UK

www.finefoodworld.co.uk/ViewPage.asp?id=30

RESOURCES

American Cheese Society

www.cheesesociety.org

Slow Food USA Presidia: American Raw Milk Cheeses

www.slowfoodusa.org/ark/raw_milk_cheese.html

Southern Foodways Alliance

www.southernfoodways.com

California Milk Advisory Board

www.realcaliforniamilk.com

National Dairy Council

www.nationaldairycouncil.org

Pacific Northwest Cheese Project

pnwcheese.typepad.com

The Great Cheeses of New England

www.newenglandcheese.com

Pennsylvania Farmstead & Artisan Cheese Alliance

www.pacheese.org

Oregon Cheese Guild
www.oregoncheeseguild.org

Maine Cheese Guild
www.mainecheeseguild.org

California Artisan Cheese Guild
www.cacheeseguild.org

The Southern Cheesemakers' Guild
www.southerncheese.com

New York State Farmstead & Artisan Cheese Makers Guild
www.nyfarmcheese.org

Vermont Institute for Artisan Cheese, University of Vermont
nutrition.uvm.edu / viac

Cal Poly Cheese, California Polytechnic State University
www.calpolycheese.com

FESTIVALS

Seattle Cheese Festival
www.seattlecheesefestival.com

Oregon Cheese Festival
www.oregoncheeseguild.org / OregonCheeseFestival.html

California's Artisan Cheese Festival
www.artisancheesefestival.com

Metric and Other Equivalencies

Imperial Measurements

Theoretically, both the United Kingdom and Canada use the metric system, but older recipes rely on the "imperial" measurement system, which differs from standard U.S. measurements in its liquid ("fluid") measurements:

¼ cup = 2.5 ounces

½ cup ("gill") = 5 ounces

1 cup = 10 ounces

1 pint = 20 ounces

1 quart = 40 ounces

Some Useful Substitutions

1 tablespoon baking powder = 2 teaspoons baking soda
+ 1 teaspoon cream of tartar

1 cup brown sugar = 1 cup white sugar + 2 tablespoons molasses

1 cup cake flour = ⅞ cup all-purpose flour + ⅛ cup cornstarch

1 cup buttermilk = 1 scant cup milk at room temperature
+ 1 tablespoon white vinegar

1 cup sour cream = 1 cup yogurt (preferably full fat)

Measurement Conversions

Note that volume (e.g., cup) measures and weight (e.g., ounce) measures convert perfectly for liquids only. Solids are a different story; 1 cup of flour weighs only 4 or 5 ounces.

Dash or pinch = less than ¼ teaspoon

3 teaspoons = 1 tablespoon

2 tablespoons = 1 fluid ounce

4 tablespoons = ¼ cup = 2 fluid ounces

16 tablespoons = 1 cup = 8 fluid ounces

2 cups = 1 pint

2 pints = 1 quart

4 quarts = 1 gallon

Imperial versus Metric

These are approximate but are fine for all uses.

1 ounce = 28 grams

1 pound = 500 grams or ½ kilogram (kilo)

2.2 pounds = 1 kilogram

1 teaspoon = 5 milliliters (mL)

1 tablespoon = 15 milliliters

1 cup = ¼ liter (L)

1 quart = 1 liter

Index

accompaniments for cheese,
32–33
Achadinha Cheese Company
(Petaluma, Calif.),
188–89
aging or ripening cheese, 19,
21–22, 39, 40, 62, 66,
85–86
Allegheny Chèvre, Crab, and
Fennel Tart, 138–39
American cheese, 35, 81
American Cheesemakers Awards,
254
American Cheese Society
(ACS), 48, 107–8,
255
awards of, 14, 57, 114, 144,
149, 161, 188–89, 249,
253–54
American Farmstead Cheese
(Kindstedt), 48

Andante Dairy (Petaluma, Calif.),
203–5
appetizers and first courses:
Baked Goat Cheese Salad,
230–31
Blue Cheese Pralines,
166–67
Cheddar Cheese Puffs, 92
Cherry Tomatoes Stuffed with
Wisconsin Herbed Cheese,
164–65
Chile con Queso "Beyond
Tex-Mex," 129
Crisp Sweetbreads on a
Fondue of Young Leeks
and Triple Cream Brie,
239–41
Escargots with Roasted Garlic
and Gorgonzola, 163
Hudson Valley Camembert
Crisp, 96–97

appetizers and first courses (*cont.*)
  Pleasant Ridge Reserve
    Farmstead Cheese with
    Crispy Serrano Ham,
    Frisée, and Candied
    Hazelnuts, 169–71
  Wild Mushroom, Requezon,
    and Epazote Quesadillas,
    242–44
  Winchester Gouda and Basil
    Gnocchi with Porcini and
    Asparagus Ragout, 236–38
Appleton Creamery (Appleton,
    Me.), 105, 106
Artisanal and Picholine, 41
artisan cheeses, 12–14, 31
ash coatings or layers, 38, 40
Asher, Gerald, 114
Asiago, makers of, 152, 197,
    199
Asparagus and Porcini Ragout,
    Winchester Gouda and
    Basil Gnocchi with,
    236–38
Auricchio (Richfield, Wis.), 151
awards, 253–55
  see also specific awards

Balsamic Syrup, 166–67
Basta, Mary, 163
Beard, James, 7, 45, 46
Beecher's Handmade Cheese
    (Seattle), 250
Behr, Ed, 110

Bellwether Farms (Valley Ford,
    Calif.), 190–91
Berkshire Blue (Great Barrington
    and Lenox, Mass.), 104,
    106
Berkshire Blue Cheese Bread
    Pudding, 102–3
Beverly Hills Cheese Shop, 41
Bice, Jennifer Lynn, 210–11
Bingham Hill, 206
Birnbaum, Chef Jan, 135–37
Biscuits, Cheddar and Chive,
    87–88
Bittersweet Plantation
    (Donaldsonville, La.),
    130–31
Bittersweet Plantation Dairy
    (Gonzales, La.), 112–13
Blackbird (Chicago), 169–71
Black Pepper Cheesecake, 98–99
BLT Fish (New York), 87
blue cheese, 21, 22, 39
  Berkshire Blue, Bread
    Pudding, 102–3
  Chipotle Dressing, 128
  Gorgonzola, Escargots with
    Roasted Garlic and, 163
  makers of, 51–52, 55–57,
    60–61, 69, 74, 104–5,
    114–18, 121, 155–56,
    160, 161–62, 181, 206,
    218–19, 221, 224, 249
  Pralines, 166–67
  Triple Walnut Dessert, 180

Boggy Meadow Farm (Walpole, N.H.), 90–91
Border Grill (Los Angeles), 233–35
Boyce, James, 221
Bravo Farms (Traver, Calif.), 249, 250
bread(s):
Cheddar and Chive Biscuits, 87–88
Cheddar and Chive Strata, 89
Farm Girl Quiche, 172–73
Provoletta, Tomato, Roasted Garlic, Oregano and Crostini, 122–24
Pudding, Berkshire Blue Cheese, 102–3
Sonoma Toast, 232
Spoon, Kentucky, with Goat Cheese and Country Ham, 176–77
Brick, makers of, 158, 160
Brie, 8, 18, 21, 23
in Blue Cheese Pralines, 166–67
makers of, 105, 221
Triple Cream, Crisp Sweetbreads on a Fondue of Young Leeks and, 239–41
Bryant, Cary, 218–19
Bubalus Bubalis (Gardena, Calif.), 250, 251

Bufala di Vermont, Vermont Water Buffalo, Inc. (South Woodstock, Vt.), 104, 105
Burros, Marian, 94–95
Burtscher, Chef Hans, 166–67
butter, 8, 33
makers of, 58, 75–76, 118, 160
buying cheese, 14–18, 43–44
author's favorite cheesemongers, 40–42

Cabot Creamery (Montpelier, Vt.), 47, 80–81, 93
Cafe Annie (Houston), 128, 129
California Goat Cheese Cheesecake, 245–46
Callahan, Cindy, 190–91
Cal Poly Creamery (San Luis Obispo, Calif.), 193–94
Camembert:
Hudson Valley, Crisp, 96–97
makers of, 61, 69, 224
Capriole Farmstead Goat Cheese (Greenville, Ind.), 109–11
Carroll, John, 45
Carroll, Ricki, 53–54, 110
Carr Valley Cheese Company (La Valle, Wis.), 155–56
Castro, Joe, 176–77
Cato Corner Farm (Colchester, Conn.), 67–68
Chalet Cheese Cooperative (Monroe, Wis.), 159–60

cheddar, 8, 14, 32, 46
    Chile con Queso "Beyond
        Tex-Mex," 129
    and Chive Biscuits, 87–88
    and Chive Strata, 89
    Chunky Cheese and Chicken
        Salad, 93
    Empty Plate Mac & Cheese,
        247
    Farm Girl Quiche, 172–73
    Macaroni and Cheese, 94–95
    makers of, 59, 61, 80–81, 84,
        85–86, 155–58, 160, 162,
        197, 199, 217
    Old-Fashioned Macaroni
        and Cheese with Crawfish,
        130–31
    A Perfect Pimento Cheese,
        140–41
    and Poblano Chile Soup with
        Crisp Cheese Crackers,
        124–27
    Puffs, 92
    Shrimp and Grits, 132–34
Cheese, Glorious Cheese! (Lambert),
    116
Cheese and Fermented Milk Foods
    (Kosikowski), 48
cheesecakes:
    Black Pepper, 98–99
    California Goat Cheese,
        245–46
Cheese Lover's Cookbook and Guide, The
    (Lambert), 116, 142–43

Cheesemaking Made Easy (Carroll), 54
cheesemongers, author's favorite,
    40–42
Cheese Shop (Carmel, Calif.), 42
Chenel, Laura, 200–202, 204,
    230–31
Cherry Tomatoes Stuffed with
    Wisconsin Herbed Cheese,
    164–65
chèvre:
    Allegheny, Crab, and Fennel
        Tart, 138–39
    Baked Goat Cheese Salad,
        230–31
    California Goat Cheese
        Cheesecake, 245–46
    Cœur à la Crème, 178–79
    makers of, 70–71, 75–76,
        111, 112–13, 115, 121,
        144, 200–202, 216–17,
        249
Chez Panisse (Berkeley, Calif.),
    200
chicken:
    and Cheese Salad, Chunky,
        93
    Chilaquiles Casserole, Green,
        233–35
    Stock, 127
Chilaquiles Casserole, Green
    Chicken, 233–35
chile:
    Chipotle–Blue Cheese
        Dressing, 128

Poblano, and Cheddar Cheese
Soup with Crisp Cheese
Crackers, 124–27
con Queso "Beyond Tex-
Mex," 129
Chipotle–Blue Cheese Dressing,
128
Chocolate Swan, The (Milwaukee
and Las Vegas), 163
Clark, Nancy and Tom, 69
Coach Farms (Pine Plains, N.Y.),
54
Cœur à la Crème, 178–79
Colby, 46, 77
makers of, 82–83, 155, 158
condiments:
Balsamic Syrup, 166–67
Candied Hazelnuts, 169, 170
Mayonnaise, 141
Oregano Oil, 122–23
Roasted Garlic, 124
Spicy Green Tomato Pickles,
135, 137
Conley, Sue, 42, 207–9
Cook, Lee, 51
Cooking for Comfort (Burros), 94–95
cooperatives, 80–81, 159–60
cost of cheese, 26–31
cottage cheese, maker of, 209
Cowgirl Creamery, 42, 207–9
cows, 26–27
Crab, Fennel, and Allegheny
Chèvre Tart, 138–39
Crackers, Crisp Cheese, 126

Crave Brothers Farmstead Cheese
(Waterloo, Wis.), 181,
182
Crawfish, Old-Fashioned
Macaroni and Cheese with,
130–31
cream cheese:
Black Pepper Cheesecake,
98–99
California Goat Cheese
Cheesecake, 245–46
Cherry Tomatoes Stuffed with
Wisconsin Herbed Cheese,
164–65
makers of, 112–13, 118,
248–49
crème fraîche, makers of, 78, 118,
191, 192, 209
Crostini, Provoletta, Tomato,
Roasted Garlic, Oregano
and, 122–24
Crowley, 46, 77
Crowley Cheese (Healdville, Vt.),
77
Cunningham, Marion, 13, 247
curds, 34
separating from whey, 10–11
Cypress Grove Chèvre (Arcata,
Calif.), 216–17

Dean & DeLuca, 41
Del Grande, Chef Robert, 128,
129
DeLuca, Giorgio, 41

desserts:

    Black Pepper Cheesecake, 98–99

    California Goat Cheese Cheesecake, 245–46

    Cœur à la Crème, 178–79

    Lemon–Goat Cheese Tart, 142–43

    Pears, Roasted Bosc, with Spiked Vermont Mascarpone, 100–101

    Triple Walnut, 180

Doel, Donna, 144

Doeling Dairy Goat Farm (Fayetteville, Ark.), 144

Doe's Leap (East Fairfield, Vt.), 104, 105

Doolan, Kristian, 104

Dressing, Chipotle–Blue Cheese, 128

Edam, maker of, 249

Edelman, Ed, 40, 46

eggs:

    Cheddar and Chive Strata, 89

    Farm Girl Quiche, 172–73

Empty Plate Mac & Cheese, 247

Epazote, Wild Mushroom, and Requezon Quesadillas, 242–44

Escargots with Roasted Garlic and Gorgonzola, 163

Fadiman, Clifton, 12

Fairway Market (New York), 40–41

Falk, Mary and Dave, 153–54

families of cheese, 21–22

Farm Girl Quiche, 172–73

farmstead cheeses, 14, 31

fat content of cheese, 8–10

Fearing, Chef Dean, 124–27

Feete family, 144

Feniger, Susan, 233–35

Fennel, Crab, and Allegheny Chèvre Tart, 138–39

festivals, 256

feta, makers of, 61, 76, 112–13, 118, 121, 156, 182, 189, 211

FireFly Farms (Bittinger, Md.), 114–15, 138–39

firm cheeses, 21, 25

first courses, *see* appetizers and first courses

Fletcher, Scott, 85–86

Fleur de Lys (San Francisco), 239–41

Folse, John, 112–13, 130–31

Fondiller, Laini, 78–79

fondue, 35

    Private Reserve, 168

fontina, maker of, 161–62

Formaggio Kitchen (Cambridge, Mass.), 41

Forman, Henry, 58

frais du sel ("fresh from the salt"),
    18
fresh cheeses, 21–22, 23, 36
fromage blanc, makers of, 75–76,
    118, 182, 191, 209, 217
Fromagerie Belle Chèvre
    (Elkmont, Ala.), 144

Gallo Family Vineyards Gold
    Medal Awards, 67, 181,
    254
Garlic, Roasted, 124
Giacomini family, 249
Gift of Southern Cooking, The (Lewis
    and Peacock), 140–41
Gillman, Mark, 67–68
Gina Marie, 249
Gingrich, Mike, 149–50
Gnocchi, Winchester Gouda and
    Basil, with Porcini and
    Asparagus Ragout, 236–38
goat cheese, 21–22, 26, 47, 148
    Baked, Salad, 230–31
    California, Cheesecake,
        245–46
    Cœur à la Crème, 178–79
    Crab, Fennel, and Allegheny
        Chèvre Tart, 138–39
    Kentucky Spoon Bread
        with Country Ham and,
        176–77
    Lemon Tart, 142–43
    makers of, 53–54, 60–61,
        70–71, 75–76, 78–79,

104, 105, 109–21, 144–
    145, 156, 182, 184, 185–
    186, 188–89, 200–205,
    210–11, 216–17, 220,
    249
    Quillisascut, in Phyllo with
        Ratatouille, 225–29
    Three-Peppercorn, Macaroni
        and, 174–75
    see also chèvre
Goat Lady Dairy (Climax, N.C.),
    144, 145
goats, 27
Golden Glen Creamery (Bow,
    Wash.), 251
Gonzalez, Mariano, 36
Gorgonzola:
    Escargots with Roasted Garlic
        and, 163
    makers of, 57, 161
Gouda, 8, 18, 22
    makers of, 59, 156, 162,
        196
    Winchester, and Basil Gnocchi
        with Porcini and Asparagus
        Ragout, 236–38
Grafton Village Cheese (Grafton,
    Vt.), 85–86, 92
Grand Hotel (Mackinac Island,
    Mich.), 166–67
Great Hill Blue (Marion, Mass.),
    104–5, 106
Green Chicken Chilaquiles
    Casserole, 233–35

Green Mountain Blue Cheese (Highgate Center, Vt.), 55–57
Gremmels, David, 218–19
Greystone Nubians (Malvern, Pa.), 70–71
Grits, Shrimp and, 132–34
grocery store cheeses, 30
Gruyère:
    makers of, 104, 161–62
    Private Reserve Fondue, 168
Gurdal, Ihsan, 41

ham:
    Country, Kentucky Spoon Bread with Goat Cheese and, 176–77
    Crispy Serrano, Pleasant Ridge Reserve Farmstead Cheese with Frisée, Candied Hazelnuts and, 169–71
hard cheeses, 21, 22, 25
Harrison, Clifford, 120
Havarti, makers of, 59, 156, 160, 162
Haystack Mountain Goat Dairy (Longmont, Colo.), 211, 249, 250
Hazelnuts, Candied, 169, 170
health concerns, 8–10, 36
Heimoff, Steve, 33
Herb Crostini, 122–23

Herbed Cheese, Wisconsin, Cherry Tomatoes Stuffed with, 164–65
Herkimer Cheese Company, 47
Home Cheesemaking (Carroll), 54
Hooper, Allison, 75–76
Hotel del Coronado (San Diego), 236–38
Hudson Valley Camembert Crisp, 96–97
Humboldt Fog, 14–17, 216

Ideal Cheese (New York), 40, 46
imperial measurements, 257, 258
Ische, Chef Greg, 236–38
Italian-style cheeses, makers of, 116–18, 151, 152, 190–191, 197–99

Jack, 14
    makers of, 81, 156, 197, 199
Jackson, Sally, 185–86
Jasper Hill Farm (Greensboro, Vt.), 74, 80
Jenkins, Steve, 40–41
Joe Matos Cheese Factory (Santa Rosa, Calif.), 214
Joe Matos St. George, in Sonoma Toast, 232

Kahan, Chef Paul, 169–71
Kaseberg, Mauney, 225
Kaufelt, Rob, 41
Keehn, Mary, 216–17

Kehler, Mateo, 74
Keller, Chef Hubert, 239–41
Keller, Chef Thomas (French
    Laundry, Per Se), 75
Kendall, Sadie, 192
Kendall Farms (Atascadero,
    Calif.), 192
Kentucky Spoon Bread with Goat
    Cheese and Country Ham,
    176–77
Kilmoyer, Letty and Bob, 60,
    110
Kindel, Peter, 211
Kindstedt, Paul, 48
Koch, Mike, 114–15
Kos Award, 48
Kosikowski, Frank, 48
Kraft, 159

La Brea Bakery (Santa Monica,
    Calif.), 41
lactose intolerance, 36
Lake Erie Creamery (Cleveland),
    181–82
Lambert, Paula, 116–18, 142–43
Laura Chenel's California Chèvre,
    200–202
Lazy Lady Farm (Westfield, Vt.),
    78–79
Lea, Lora, 220, 225
leaves, cheeses wrapped in, 38
Leeks, Young, Crisp Sweetbreads
    on a Fondue of Triple
    Cream Brie and, 239–41

Lemon–Goat Cheese Tart,
    142–43
L'Etoile (Madison, Wis.), 178–79
Liederkranz, 159
Limburger, maker of, 159–60
Little, Jeremy, 120–21
Loews Miami Beach Hotel, 122
LoveTree Farmstead Cheese
    (Grantsburg, Wis.),
    153–54

MacAlister, Elizabeth, 67–68
macaroni:
    and Cheese, 94–95
    and Cheese, Old-Fashioned,
        with Crawfish, 130–31
    Empty Plate Mac & Cheese,
        247
    and Three-Peppercorn Goat
        Cheese, 174–75
main courses:
    Berkshire Blue Cheese Bread
        Pudding, 102–3
    Cheddar and Chive Strata, 89
    Chunky Cheese and Chicken
        Salad, 93
    Crab, Fennel, and Allegheny
        Chèvre Tart, 138–39
    Empty Plate Mac & Cheese,
        247
    Farm Girl Quiche, 172–73
    Green Chicken Chilaquiles
        Casserole, 233–35
    Macaroni and Cheese, 94–95

main courses (*cont.*)

    Macaroni and Three-
      Peppercorn Goat Cheese,
      174–75

    Oven-Roasted Raclette with
      Sausage, Potatoes, and
      Pickled Green Tomatoes,
      135–37

    Pleasant Ridge Reserve
      Farmstead Cheese with
      Crispy Serrano Ham,
      Frisée, and Candied
      Hazelnuts, 169–71

    Private Reserve Fondue,
      168

    Provoletta, Tomato, Roasted
      Garlic, Oregano, and
      Crostini, 122–24

    Quillisascut Goat Cheese in
      Phyllo with Ratatouille,
      225–29

    Shrimp and Grits, 132–34

    Winchester Gouda and Basil
      Gnocchi with Porcini and
      Asparagus Ragout,
      236–38

Major, Cindy, 62–66, 74

Major, David, 62–66

Malakasis, Tasia, 144

Mansion on Turtle Creek (Dallas),
    124–27

Marin French Cheese Company
    (Petaluma, Calif.), 18,
    221–24

mascarpone:

    California Goat Cheese
      Cheesecake, 245–46

    makers of, 75–76, 116–18,
      181

    Spiked Vermont, Roasted
      Bosc Pears with, 100–101

Mason, Fanny, 90–91

Matos, Joe, 214

Mayonnaise, 141

Maytag Dairy Farms (Newton,
    Iowa), 180, 181, 182

McCalman, Max, 41

McDaniel, Chef Caroline,
    132–34

Meadow Creek Dairy (Galax, Va.),
    144

measurement conversions,
    257–58

Menhennett Farms (Cochranville,
    Pa.), 51–52

Meriweather, Annette, 51–52

metric measurements, 258

Mexican-style cheeses:

    Green Chicken Chilaquiles
      Casserole, 233–35

    makers of, 116–18

Miller, Chef Tory, 178–79

Milliken, Mary Sue, 233–35

Misterly, Rick, 220

mold, 20, 25, 38, 39

Monterey Jack, makers of, 81,
    156, 199

Morin-Boucher, Dawn, 55–57

mozzarella, 3, 43–44
    buffalo's milk, 184, 249–50
    makers of, 81, 116–18, 151,
        181, 184, 249–50
Mozzarella Company (Dallas),
    116–18
Muenster, makers of, 81, 160
Murray's Cheese (New York),
    41
mushroom(s):
    Porcini and Asparagus
        Ragout, Winchester Gouda
        and Basil Gnocchi with,
        236–38
    wild, in Berkshire Blue Cheese
        Bread Pudding, 102–3
    Wild, Requezon, and Epazote
        Quesadillas, 242–44
Myrdal, Amy, 172–73

Nantwich International Cheese
    Show, 255
Neal's Yard Dairy, 42
Newbold, Douglass, 70–71
New England Cheesemaking
    Supply Company (Ashfield,
    Mass.), 53–54
nibbles:
    Sonoma Toast, 232
    see also appetizers and first
        courses

Oakville Grocery (San Francisco),
    1–4, 43–44

Old Chatham Sheepherding
    Company (Old Chatham,
    N.Y.), 69, 96–97
Olson, Myron, 159–60
Orb Weaver Farm (New Haven,
    Vt.), 54, 82–83
Oregano Oil, 122–23

Pacheco, Donna and Jim,
    188–89
Pampano (New York), 242
Parmesan, makers of, 151, 152
Parnell, Elizabeth, 144
pasta:
    Winchester Gouda and Basil
        Gnocchi with Porcini and
        Asparagus Ragout, 236–38
    see also macaroni
Pasta Shop (Oakland and Berkeley,
    Calif.), 42
pasteurization, 36–38
Peacock, Chef Scott, 140–41
pears:
    Roasted Bosc, with Spiked
        Vermont Mascarpone,
        100–101
    Triple Walnut Dessert, 180
pecans, in Blue Cheese Pralines,
    166–67
Peluso, Franklin, 193–94
pepper(corn):
    Black, Cheesecake, 98–99
    Three-, Goat Cheese,
        Macaroni and, 174–75

peppers:
    A Perfect Pimento Cheese,
        140–41
    roasting and peeling, 140–41
phyllo:
    Hudson Valley Camembert
        Crisp, 96–97
    Quillisascut Goat Cheese in,
        with Ratatouille, 225–29
Pickles, Spicy Green Tomato, 135,
    137
Pimento Cheese, A Perfect,
    140–41

Plasse, Chantal, 110
plastic vacuum packs, 39–40
plastic wrap, 19, 20
Pleasant Ridge Reserve, 149–50
    Farmstead Cheese with Crispy
        Serrano Ham, Frisée,
        and Candied Hazelnuts,
        169–71
Pleasant Valley Dairy (Ferndale,
    Wash.), 251
Poblano Chile and Cheddar
    Cheese Soup with Crisp
    Cheese Crackers, 124–27
Point Reyes Original Blue (Point
    Reyes Station, Calif.), 249,
    250
Pollack, Marian, 82–83
Porcini and Asparagus Ragout,
    Winchester Gouda and
    Basil Gnocchi with, 236–
    238

potato(es):
    Gnocchi, Winchester Gouda
        and Basil, with Porcini and
        Asparagus Ragout, 236–38
    Oven-Roasted Raclette with
        Sausage, Pickled Green
        Tomatoes and, 135–37
    Soup, Creamy, 90–91
Pralines, Blue Cheese, 166–67
Private Reserve Fondue, 168
process cheese, 35
Provoletta, Tomato, Roasted
    Garlic, Oregano, and
    Crostini, 122–24
provolone, maker of, 151
Puffs, Cheddar Cheese, 92
Putnam, John and Janine,
    49–50

quark, maker of, 75–76
Quatrano, Anne, 120
Quesadillas, Wild Mushroom,
    Requezon, and Epazote,
    242–44
Quiche, Farm Girl, 172–73
Quillisascut Cheese Company
    (Rice, Wash.), 220
Quillisascut Goat Cheese in Phyllo
    with Ratatouille, 225–29

raclette, 35
    Oven-Roasted, with Sausage,
        Potatoes, and Pickled
        Green Tomatoes, 135–37

Rance, Patrick, 66
Raspberry Sauce, 178, 179
Ratatouille, Quillisascut Goat
        Cheese in Phyllo with,
        225–29
Rautureau, Chef Thierry, 225–29
raw milk cheeses, 36–38
        makers of, 154, 191
Redwood Hill Farm and Creamery
        (Sebastopol, Calif.),
        210–11
Reese, Bob, 75–76
rennet, 34
Requezon, Wild Mushroom,
        and Epazote Quesadillas,
        242–44
ricotta, 10
        makers of, 69, 118, 191
rinds, eating, 38, 40
ripening, see aging or ripening
        cheese
Rogue Creamery (Central Point,
        Oreg.), 218–19
Rosewood Mansion (Dallas),
        245–46
Roth Käse, 161–62, 168
Rover's (Seattle), 225–29

salads:
        Baked Goat Cheese, 230–31
        Chipotle–Blue Cheese
                Dressing for, 128
        Chunky Cheese and Chicken,
                93

Pleasant Ridge Reserve
        Farmstead Cheese with
        Crispy Serrano Ham,
        Frisée, and Candied
        Hazelnuts, 169–71
Sally Jackson Cheeses (Oroville,
        Wash.), 185–86
Salsa, Tomatillo, 235
Salsa Verde, 243
salt content of cheese, 10
Samish Bay Cheese (Bow, Wash.),
        251
Samuelsson, Chef Marcus,
        98–99
Sancerre Sauce, 226, 228
Sandoval, Chef Richard,
        242–44
Santacrus, Josefina, 242
sauces:
        Chile con Queso "Beyond
                Tex-Mex," 129
        Chipotle–Blue Cheese
                Dressing, 128
        Raspberry, 178, 179
        Sancerre, 226, 228
Sausage, Oven-Roasted Raclette
        with Potatoes, Pickled
        Green Tomatoes and,
        135–37
Scanlan, Soyoung, 203–5
Schad, Judy, 109–11
seafood:
        Crab, Fennel, and Allegheny
                Chèvre Tart, 138–39

seafood (*cont.*)

    Crawfish, Old-Fashioned
Macaroni and Cheese with,
130–31

    Escargots with Roasted Garlic
and Gorgonzola, 163

    Shrimp and Grits, 132–34

Sebastiani, Jim, 5

semi-firm cheeses, 21, 25

semi-soft cheeses, 21, 22, 24–25,
39

serving cheese, 20

sheep, 27–30

sheep's milk cheeses, 21, 22,
26

    makers of, 51–52, 62–66,
69, 105, 155–56, 184,
185–86, 190–91

Shelburne Farms (Shelburne, Vt.),
66, 84

Shrimp and Grits, 132–34

side dishes:

    Cheddar and Chive Biscuits,
87–88

    Kentucky Spoon Bread with
Goat Cheese and Country
Ham, 176–77

    Macaroni and Cheese,
94–95

Sierra Nevada (Willows, Calif.),
248–49, 250

Silverton, Nancy, 41

Smith, Dave, 58–59

Smith, Peggy, 42, 207–9

Smith's Country Cheese
(Winchendon, Mass.),
58–59

Smokejacks (Burlington, Vt.), 46,
84

soft and soft-ripened cheeses, 21,
23–24, 39, 40

SoHo Grand Hotel (New York), 94

Solanet, Pablo, 114–15, 138–39

Sonoma Toast, 232

Sophie's Cellars (Monte Rio,
Calif.), 206

soups:

    Cheddar Cheese and Poblano
Chile, with Crisp Cheese
Crackers, 124–27

    Potato, Creamy, 90–91

specialty cheeses, 12, 30–31

Spoon Bread, Kentucky, with Goat
Cheese and Country Ham,
176–77

Star Provisions (Atlanta), 120–21

starters, in cheesemaking, 34

Stella Cheese Company, 152

Stetson, Bob, 60–61

Stock, Chicken, 127

storing cheese, 19–20, 23–26

Stornetta Dairy (Sonoma, Calif.),
200–202

Strata, Cheddar and Chive, 89

Straus Family Creamery, 33

string cheese, makers of, 116–18,
160, 181

Susman, Marjorie, 82–83

Sweetbreads, Crisp, on a Fondue
of Young Leeks and Triple
Cream Brie, 239–41
Sweet Grass Dairy (Thomasville,
Ga.), 120–21
Swiss cheese:
Creamy Potato Soup, 90–91
makers of, 81, 156, 160,
162
Syrup, Balsamic, 166–67

Tamayo (Denver), 242–44
tarts:
Crab, Fennel, and Allegheny
Chèvre, 138–39
Lemon–Goat Cheese, 142–43
tastings, 3–4
Tea and Tarot (Sebastopol, Calif.),
232
teleme, maker of, 193–94
terroir, 33
Tesar, Chef John, 245–46
Thistle Hill Farm (North
Pomfret, Vt.), 49–50
Three Mountain Inn (Jamaica,
Vt.), 89
Three Sisters Farmstead (Lindsay,
Calif.), 249, 250
Tomales Bay Foods (Point Reyes
Station, Calif.), 42, 207,
209
tomatillo(s):
Salsa, 235
Salsa Verde, 243

tomato(es):
Cherry, Stuffed with
Wisconsin Herbed Cheese,
164–65
Confit, 124
Pickles, Spicy Green, 135,
137
tortilla chips, in Chile con Queso
"Beyond Tex-Mex," 129
tortillas, in Green Chicken
Chilaquiles Casserole,
233–35
Tourondel, Chef Laurent, 87–88
Traders Point Creamery
(Zionsville, Ind.), 144
Triballat family, 200–202
triple cream cheeses:
Brie, Crisp Sweetbreads on a
Fondue of Young Leeks
and, 239–41
makers of, 112–13, 118, 205,
221, 224
Triple Walnut Dessert, 180

Uplands Cheese Company
(Dodgeville, Wis.), 149–50

Van Vlaaderen, George, 104
Vella, Ig, 161, 197–99, 218
Vella, Tom, 218
Vella Cheese Company (East
Sonoma, Calif.), 197–99
Velveeta, in Chile con Queso
"Beyond Tex-Mex," 129

Vermont Butter & Cheese Company (Websterville, Vt.), 33, 75–76, 100–101
Vermont Shepherd (Putney, Vt.), 62–66

walnut(s):
 Blue Cheese Pralines, 166–67
 Triple, Dessert, 180
Washington State University Creamery (Pullman, Wash.), 251
water buffalo cheese, makers of, 184, 249–50
Waters, Alice, 200
waxed paper, 19–20
wax wrappings, 38
Wehner family, 121
Weinzweig, Ari, 41
Wesselink, Jules, 195–96
Westfield Farm (Hubbardston, Mass.), 60–61, 110
whey, 34
 separating curds from, 10–11
Whole Foods, 14–17
Widmer's Cheese Cellars (Theresa, Wis.), 157–58, 164–65
Willamette Valley Cheese (Salem, Oreg.), 251
Winchester Cheese Company (Winchester, Calif.), 195–96

Winchester Gouda and Basil Gnocchi with Porcini and Asparagus Ragout, 236–38
wine:
 pairing cheese and, 32–33
 Private Reserve Fondue, 168
 Roasted Bosc Pears with Spiked Vermont Mascarpone, 100–101
 Sancerre Sauce, 226, 228
Wine Journey along the Russian River, A (Heimoff), 32–33
Wisconsin Cheese Makers Association awards, 254
Wölffer Estate Vineyard (Sagaponack, N.Y.), 104, 105
World Cheese Awards, 218, 221, 255
wrappings, 38

yogurt, makers of, 104, 144, 211
York Hill Farm (New Sharon, Me.), 105, 106
young cheeses, 18
Yturriondobeitia, Jaime, 84

Zingerman's Deli and Roadhouse (Ann Arbor, Mich.), 41, 54, 174–75

Made in the USA
Middletown, DE
02 June 2016